Selling Your Dolls
and Teddy Bears

Selling Your Dolls & Teddy Bears

Barb Lawrence Giguere and
Carol-Lynn Rössel Waugh

BETTERWAY BOOKS
CINCINNATI, OHIO

Other fine Betterway Books are available from your local bookstore or direct from the publisher.

01   00   99   98   97   5   4   3   2   1

Library of Congress Cataloging-in-Publication Data

Giguere, Barb Lawrence
    Selling your dolls and teddy bears / by Barb Lawrence Giguere and Carol-Lynn Rössel Waugh.
        p.   cm.
    Includes index.
    ISBN 1-55870-439-6
    1. Doll industry—Management. 2. Toy industry—Management. 3. New business enterprises—Management. 4. Doll—Marketing. 5. Teddy bears—Marketing. 6. Stuffed animals (Toys)—Marketing. I. Waugh, Carol-Lynn Rössel. II. Title.
HD9993.D652G54   1996
745.592'21'0688—dc20   96-42196
                                                                                      CIP

Edited by Argie J. Manolis
Production edited by Jennifer Lepore
Interior and cover designed by Sandy Kent
Cover illustration by Gay W. Holland

Barb
Lawrence Giguere

Barb Lawrence Giguere didn't know she was a teddy bear artist until she was halfway through writing this book. She didn't know she was a doll artist until she turned a sculpture into a doll in 1986—although she had been designing and making dolls and bears since her first child was born in 1966. Yet, she had been preparing for these job descriptions most of her life. She studied art for twelve years at the prestigious Maine College of Art, earned a bachelors degree in mechanical engineering from the University of New Hampshire, and a bachelors and masters degree in business administration from the University of Maine. In 1992, she pulled all these facets of her training together to found the Maine Society of Doll and Bear Artists, Inc., an organization with a vital, growing international juried membership. Barb believes that one must visualize her dreams, and then dedicate herself to them, and this philosophy has helped her achieve great things in every business endeavor she's chosen in life. She has thoroughly researched every aspect of her business and is dedicated to helping those around her reach the height of their abilities. She believes in building confidence in others. Her rapid rise to the stature of "industry expert" shows she knows what she's talking (and writing) about. Barb lives in Scarborough, Maine.

Carol-Lynn
Rössel Waugh

Artist/writer/photographer Carol-Lynn Rössel Waugh coined the term "teddy bear artist" in the early 1980s to describe the work she and a handful of American doll artists were creating. Her many published books, articles and photographs, and her handmade and commercially produced teddy bears and dolls, including crowd-pleasers like "Yetta Nother Bear" and "Gregory," have brought her international fame. She has been in the doll business since 1972, the year she moved to Maine from her native New York, but she has been designing dolls and doll clothes since she was six. Carol-Lynn insists that her bears are "furry dolls." When collectors ask how she so well captures the essence of childhood joy and innocence in her work, she answers, "I just make what I want to play with." Carol-Lynn lives in Winthrop, Maine.

Dedication

To our colleagues in the Maine Society of Doll and Bear Artists, who will recognize themselves in these pages. Thank you for sharing yourselves and your art.

Acknowledgments

Thank you, Argie, for your patience, understanding, friendship and perseverance.

TABLE OF CONTENTS

INTRODUCTION

It's a jungle out there.

If you've ever tried to sell your dolls or teddies in today's marketplace, you know what we're talking about. Shows nowadays are top-heavy with artists and artisans, all vying for the ever tighter purses of a picky public. Shops seem to be buying safe or name brand products. And full-color magazine ads—which some consider to be the key to mail-order sales— are just too expensive. With these obstacles to climb, how can you and your product stand out, be seen and sell?

You need to learn marketing techniques. You are probably thinking, "I don't have time to learn abstract business terms or social sciences. I need to spend my time creating."

OK. As long as you can hang onto that rich patron or inheritance, you're right. But we're assuming that, since you've picked up this book, you're trying to sell your dolls or teddy bears, and—just maybe—you're a tad lost in that jungle we mentioned.

You're not alone. We were lost too when we started back in the 1970s and 1980s. Of course, the art doll and bear markets were nothing like today's. There *was* no art bear market then! But that doesn't mean it was any easier to crack. True, there were fewer artists. But there were even fewer collectors and fewer retailers offering artist originals! People would look at our original porcelain dolls and ask where we bought heads, or inquire, "Which pattern did you use for this bear?" (OK, people still do that today, but you get the idea.)

All we needed was a plan—a road map—as well as a lot of determination and a positive approach. And it's been working. How do we know? In 1992, nobody in the doll world had ever heard of Barb, yet she'd been selling her original dolls for years. By 1995, she had received major coverage in four top doll magazines, and her name was on everyone's lips. And— best of all—her work is selling throughout the U.S., Canada and Europe. Carol-Lynn has been involved in the doll and bear markets since their early beginnings, and has been very successful at marketing herself and selling her dolls and bears to collectors *and* marketing her designs to manu- facturers. Sound good? Then bear (doll?) with us. Let us be your guides into the sometimes overwhelming world of selling yourself as well as your work.

This book is constructed so you can turn to the section of the map that will take you where you most want to go right now. Part 1 will help you research the market, establish your business, define your product and deal with finances. Part 2 will help you publicize your business and yourself, offering tips on marketing yourself, gaining name recognition, putting together a press kit and press releases, photographing your creations, and advertising. Part 3 will give you advice on selling through direct mail, through retail and trade shows, to shops and to manufacturers.

You say you know how to set up a good sales booth, but you can't seem to attract customers? Turn to chapters 5 and 13 for advice on developing an image for yourself and your business and selling at shows. If you've been selling at shows, but are spending too much time and money traveling and want to try other sales options, turn to chapter 11 for advice on selling by direct mail, or chapter 14, selling wholesale to doll and teddy bear shops. If you're interested in having your designs mass-produced, check out chapter 15 for insider information on getting commercial contracts with the right manufacturers. Do you want to make your name a household word? This is harder, but we'll tell *all*. You just might find yourself having to hide at shows because complete strangers know who you are—and expect you to know them, too!

We want to emphasize from the beginning that we are not fairy god-mothers, merely native guides. There's no guarantee that, instantly, after reading our words, you'll find fame and fortune. That depends on work, dedication, talent, determination, perseverance and—sometimes most important—dumb luck.

So, are you ready for an adventure? Glance at the table of contents. Decide what route you want to follow. And leave the guiding to us!

PART ONE

Getting Started

CHAPTER ONE

Researching Your Field

Whether you have been making dolls and teddy bears for years or are just beginning, it is imperative you keep abreast of what is going on in your field. This should not only be your first step when starting a business, it should be a habit, a way of life, that will continually add to your success. Whatever business you're in, you must know who's who. Know your customers. Know the trends. Know your sources. Know where to find information. This may sound like a monumental task, but you really must do this while still making and selling your creations.

KNOWING THE PLAYERS

Your own studio and product is part of a vast industry. To succeed in this business, you need to know the products and the players—the dolls, teddies and humans! The best way to do this is to study all the major doll and teddy bear magazines on the market. Get to know names that appear and reappear. *The Teddy Bear Sourcebook* and *The Doll Sourcebook*, both published by Betterway Books, will give you an excellent overview of the market.

The more you know, the better your chances for competing in this overcrowded marketplace. Learn about other artists. Who is working in which mediums? Who makes miniature bears and who makes large toddler-sized teddies? Which artists are working exclusively in polymers? Who sculpts directly into porcelain clay? What materials are artists using for costuming? Learn who is doing what and for whom. Which artists are teaching classes and seminars? Which artists are attending signings at shops? Which artists are attending certain shows?

Study shop advertisements. Which shops are selling only artist-made originals? Which shops are buying which dolls and teddy bears? Some shops only deal in one-of-a-kind dolls and bears or in a certain price range. Listings in sourcebooks and ads will give you an overview of the types of dolls and bears each shop sells.

While you are at it, study manufacturers' ads as well. They will teach you quite a bit about advertising campaigns. Pinpoint how your dolls or bears are different. These are aspects of your creations on which you can capitalize.

If you study old magazines, you will be surprised at how quickly names come and go. It takes hard work and determination to succeed in the doll or bear world, just as in every other field. When you're working alone, you wear all the hats—all the jobs are your responsibility. How can you possibly do all this research and make dolls or teddy bears too?

MANAGING YOUR TIME

Incorporate time management into each day. You know by now that making dolls and teddy bears is an obsessive, all-consuming activity. You won't want to do anything else or discuss anything not doll or teddy bear related. But every so often, you will need a break from your creative work. Take this time for research. Photocopy articles to which you'll want to refer later. Placing these in file folders or in a three-ring notebook as soon as you find them will save a lot of time you would later be spending searching for elusive pages. Use index cards, a Rolodex, or enter information about retailers into a computer database. Anything that keeps you from your doll making or teddy bear making will soon become annoying, especially when you're getting ready for a show or trying to fill an order, so keeping up with research will save time later.

ATTENDING SHOWS AS A CUSTOMER

If you have never sold your creations at a show, or if show sales are generally slow for you, try attending some shows as a customer to give you the time necessary to really see how others are selling their teddies and dolls. (You can also do this at shows where you are exhibiting if you bring someone along to run your booth.) Attend all kinds of shows—doll shows, teddy bear shows, juried craft shows—any show where artists and artisans are selling handmade items. Notice why some people seem to be selling while others are not.

Attending shows is a great way to learn about presentation. You'll learn that successful artists are constantly talking to prospective customers rather than hiding behind their booths. Take notes. Use a pocket tape recorder to record your thoughts. (Do not use a video camera, as other artists may worry that you are trying to steal their designs.) Do whatever it takes to learn more about who is selling what and how they are doing so.

Take notes on the types of items sold and how they are displayed. Look at other artists' sales tools. Write everything down, even if it seems insignificant. The more you notice, the more you learn! It's always better, if possible, to attend a show as a customer before you decide to invest the necessary money to do the show yourself.

Attending shows is also a great networking tool. Introduce yourself to artists whom you have never met, and talk to those you know. Share knowledge as freely as you ask questions. You will quickly learn you have entered a wonderfully giving world of artists, show promoters, shop owners, suppliers and others. The success of each depends on the others. Most will be eager to find another soul to talk with about their bears or dolls.

Artists tend to be hermit-like, yet crave input from others. Learn about other artists' work. Share yours with them. Some of the best critiques you'll get will be from other artists. Most of us have experienced the same problems. There's nothing more rewarding than having another artist praise your work!

CHAPTER TWO

Establishing Your Company

ompany? What company, you ask? Your company. If you are selling teddy bears or dolls for money, or intend to do so, you have to become a company. There is an unfortunate perception that artists and artisans are not business people. This perception makes it all the more important that you present yourself professionally.

If you haven't formed a company, we'll start from the beginning by helping you choose a company name and logo and register your business. If you already have a business, this chapter will offer additional ideas and insight, help you organize your business expenses for the ever-dreaded tax time, and give you information on establishing a professional image, using a computer, and making decisions about legal concerns such as trademarking your name and logo or incorporating your business.

CHOOSING A COMPANY NAME

There are two approaches to naming your company: using your own name as your business name or creating another name for your business. Each has its advantages and disadvantages. One thing is certain: You don't want to be confused with someone else or another business.

Using your own name simplifies things. There probably isn't another doll or teddy bear artist with your name. But, there is one considerable advantage to having a business name. Using a business name different from your own allows you to share booth or table space at the larger, more established shows. Confused? Many shows do not allow artists to share space. Other promoters only permit a limited number of artists' names assigned to any one booth or table. It's not easy to prove you are two or more people; but if you have a business name, you can represent the work of other artists. This helps cut costs at the larger, more expensive shows.

It will take some time and research to choose a name capturing the uniqueness of your work, and one no one else is using. You may want your business name to *say* you're selling dolls or bears. You may want to indicate the area you're from by tapping into the romance of the area, or use your children's or grandchildren's names or a nickname. Don't select a name that is difficult to pronounce, nor one that's too long. You can always add descriptive wording to business cards, hangtags, brochures and advertisements.

Carol-Lynn uses her name as her business name and has been happy with this for over twenty years. Barb uses the business name, Memories and Smiles. . . . She selected this name because collectors always smile at her work and seem to exclaim, "Look! This doll reminds me of . . ." a specific someone.

Adding "& Company" to your business name often indicates that the teddy bears or dolls are made by more than one person. When demand increases and a cottage industry develops to supply that demand, this may be necessary.

There is no right or wrong way to choose a business name. You can change a business name, but it's best to choose one and stay with it. You will use your business name to register your business locally, in your state, when applying for permits and sales/use tax identification numbers, on correspondence, business cards, hangtags and in advertisements.

CREATING A LOGO

Along with your business name, you may want to use a logo. Your logo should be unique, something that collectors and dealers visually associate with you. Many artists do not use one, and it is not a necessity. But if you do decide to use one, take time developing it. Look through magazines or newspapers. What are other people using? This is where the research you did earlier—including articles and ads you have clipped from magazines— will come in handy. Don't limit your research to the doll or teddy bear worlds. Logos are everywhere. Look through the yellow pages. Think about logos you easily recognize—the logo for the American Automobile Association is a good one. Think about what makes them easily recognizable. Usually they are fairly simple images or symbols that can be easily associated with a company.

Avoid the "common" images people use for logos, like bear paw prints for teddy bear artists. Stay away from busy logos that overpower the words. Don't borrow from someone else's logo, it might be trademarked or copyright protected.

Barb spent nearly thirty years trying to create a unique look using her

Barb Giguere's logo consists of her initials, *B, L* and *G*, intertwined.

Jacques Dorier created his logo using his signature. Jacques is written inside the large *D* of Dorier. The signature is turned on its side. Someone told Jacques that his signature looked like his profile, so he added a nose (in red, so as not to be confused with the signature). The border around his profile is also red. Alongside the signature are his name and company name in simple type.

Monika's logo is a uniquely styled *M* with her name beneath it.

Lee Middleton Original Dolls, Inc., uses a graphical logo.

initials. She wanted to interconnect them in some way. One day she drew exactly what she wanted—a *B, L* and *G* intertwined, each letter using a part of another. Carol-Lynn uses a heart as her logo. Every one of her dolls and bears wears a heart. Some wear a tiny heart charm. Others wear custom-made heart-shaped pins.

You say you aren't a graphic designer, and you can't afford to hire one to design your logo? Don't despair. There are many clip art designs that are copyright free. North Light Books of Cincinnati, Ohio and Dover Publications of New York publish books containing available clip art designs. These are usually available through art and craft supply stores.

Select designs that interest you and photocopy them. Mix and match.

Cut and paste. Enlarge and shrink. You'll be surprised how much fun you're having and how much you enjoy this new creative outlet.

Once you've finalized your logo, make copies of it in different sizes. Include your new logo on your business cards, letterheads, envelopes, postcards, hangtags, sewn-in labels and in all your advertisements. If you want the public to recognize your logo, you have to use it!

If you're an experienced quilter or have experience doing silk screen designs, or know someone who is, put your logo on a banner for use at shows. It doesn't have to be large. An 18″ × 36″ banner is a perfect size to hang against a backdrop or in front of a table.

USING A COMPUTER

As you establish your business, you will find more and more uses for a computer. Today they are fairly affordable through discount office supply stores and computer shows. If you decide to purchase a computer, take your time choosing the system and programs right for you. Some features you might want to consider include: a word processing program for correspondence, a database program for mailing lists and keeping track of sales and business expenses, and a desktop publishing program that will allow you to put images on the page. You might also want to consider a modem to allow you to connect to the Internet and send and receive faxes, and a flatbed color scanner to facilitate creating your own advertising flyers.

If you cannot afford a computer or do not want to purchase one immediately, you can often use computers for an hourly fee at your local library, or at copy centers that offer twenty-four-hour access. They have employees who can do the keyboard work for you while you select the look you want. They will allow you to save what you have done to a diskette for future use.

ESTABLISHING A PROFESSIONAL IMAGE

As your business grows, you will want to acquire business tools like stationery and envelopes, receipt books and other items with your business name and logo on them. You may want to consider a fax machine for ease in sending and receiving orders and correspondence. Shop around. Office supply stores and computer shows often offer them at discount prices.

Some computer software may allow you to create a business image at a cost far less than using the services of graphic designers, advertising specialists and printers. Using pre-designed borders, scenes and other special looks for stationery or business cards can enhance your professional image.

Establish your credibility. Many people do not take artists seriously in the business world. You have to work to be recognized as a legitimate business person as well as an artist. Those buying artist-made original dolls and teddies want to buy from successful artists. The more business tools you use, the more time you spend establishing your business in the early stages, the better your sales will be!

REGISTERING YOUR BUSINESS

It is smart to formally register your business name. This is a very simple matter in most communities. For a small filing fee (Barb's was only five dollars), you register your business name, yourself as the owner, your address and what the business does with your city or town government. You might have to assure your community that you won't be running a retail shop in a residential zone or you aren't planning to turn your home into a manufacturing facility.

By applying for a Sales and Use Tax Permit, you are registering your business with each state in which you intend to sell your dolls and bears. You'll need to do this in advance of selling at retail shows in each state. Beware: This does not prevent others in that state from using the same business name. Only incorporation gives you this protection.

TRADEMARKING YOUR LOGO AND NAME

You may decide to protect your logo and company name so others cannot use it. Protecting them through trademark can be a sound business decision.

Trademark is defined as any word, name, symbol or any combination thereof used by a merchant or manufacturer of a product to identify his or her goods and to distinguish them from the products of competitors.

Trademarks must be used at the point of sale. A trademark may be placed in any manner on products, their containers, hangtags or in advertisements. Trademarks do not have to be physically attached to the goods, but they do have to be associated with the product at the point of sale.

Once a trademark has been adopted and used, it falls under the purview of common law trademark protection. This protects the owner against another person using a confusingly similar trademark.

Greater protection is available under federal and state statutes. The federal statute is known as the Lanham Trade-Mark Act of 1946, and it provides a clearing house for existing trademarks through its registration process. To apply for federal registration, you must state a legitimate intent to use the mark in commerce or in connection with goods in commerce. The applications are reviewed by employees of the Patent and Trademark

Office. They look for similar trademarks in the application stage and those already registered. If none are found, they will publish your mark in the *Official Gazette of the U.S. Patent and Trademark Office* and anyone who objects may do so within thirty days. An objection must have merit.

You have six months after receiving a notice of allowance to provide the Patent and Trademark Office with a statement that the trademark is in commercial use. You will also have to provide them with a drawing of the mark, three facsimiles or specimens of the trademark as it is being used in connection with the goods in commerce, and the filing fee of $175.

State trademark statutes are similar to those of the Lanham Act. A few grant even further protection, but they do not extend beyond the borders of the state in which they are filed. Applications are filed with the state office of trademarks, and they require documentation similar to federal registration.

Ask yourself if trademark protection is worth the cost of developing the mark and registering it. If you hire a lawyer, you must add legal expenses as well. Trademark registration is good for ten years. Then you must reapply. Costs can easily reach one thousand dollars.

TAXES AND TAX RECORDS

The earlier you start thinking about taxes, the better. There are many different approaches doll and teddy bear artists can use when filing taxes. This will not be a popular statement, but we must make it anyway: Few accountants acknowledge we are "in business" when it comes to making dolls and teddy bears. After all, aren't we all just adults trying to regain our lost childhoods?

If you have your taxes done by tax services or accountants, take charge of your business by deciding which reporting method is best for you. There are several different tax categories. Most doll and teddy bear artists find a Schedule C works best.

This form does change some from year to year, but it is fairly consistent. Before you set up your bookkeeping, request a Schedule C from your local Internal Revenue Service Office. Use the expense classifications for your own bookkeeping. Barb had to laugh when one artist came to her in tears. The artist couldn't decide where to record some of her expenses because there wasn't a space for them. The government doesn't make special forms for doll and teddy bear artists! Use common sense and you'll realize booth rental at shows is an advertising expense. So are photographs and postage to mail them to potential customers.

Here is a list of business expenses to consider for tax purposes:

COMPUTING MILEAGE

Keep a small notebook with you in your car to record mileage to and from shows, to and from trips to get supplies, drop off film or pick up photos or slides of your work, and any other travel related to doing business. List the date, the beginning and ending mileage, along with the starting point, destination and ending point. Compute miles traveled. Circle this. You will be amazed how many business-related miles you travel each year. This is another figure you can use when computing your taxes and costs of doing business.

- Photographs of your work, including the cost of film and processing or professional photographs. If you've purchased a camera or special lenses because you want to do your own photography, include one-fourth of these expenses. Classify these under advertising expenses.
- Actual costs for business cards, stationery, envelopes, rubber stamps, printed forms, flyers or brochures, and postage you use during that year. If you have five hundred forms printed but only use one hundred, compute the cost for one hundred.
- Business card holder, table covers, shelving, risers, display items, decorations for booth display, lighting and light bulbs, and any other items purchased for use at shows.
- Booth/table rental, as well as any additional costs for electricity, additional tables, etc.
- Telephone calls made for business purposes. Take time to photocopy your phone bills and identify which calls are business related.
- One-fifth of the cost of a word processor, computer, printer or facsimile machine purchased for your business.
- Annual magazine subscriptions, books and other publications related to running your business.
- Mileage acquired while doing business. Multiply the mileage by $.35 for your annual vehicle expenses.
- Advertising expenses.
- Business-related legal or accounting fees.
- Dues to professional organizations.
- Any other business-related expenses.

All legitimate business expenses must be verifiable for tax purposes. Keep good records. Keep receipts when applicable. These are the necessary steps you must take to make tax time bearable!

WHAT ABOUT INCORPORATING?

We are strong believers in controlling our own business decisions. Most bookstores carry books on starting your own business and incorporating. Look for those pertaining to artists and craftspeople.

Incorporating shouldn't be a consideration until you're making $30,000 or more per year from the sale of your dolls and bears. This is the figure where tax advantages take effect. If you decide on incorporation but can't afford the costs involved, contact The Company Corporation in Delaware at (800) 542-2677. Their business is to incorporate your business.

CHAPTER THREE

Making Your Dolls and Bears the Best They Can Be

*H*ave you ever watched collectors at their first doll or teddy bear show? They are in awe. By the time they've gone halfway through the show, they're totally confused. The closest many of them have ever come to seeing so many dolls and teddies in person at one time might be (horrors!) a toy store! Perhaps they never realized there is an artist behind every creation. Their collections may consist entirely of *manufactured* dolls or teddy bears. They had no idea there were so many ways dolls and bears could vary. They love everything. But everything is blending together in their minds. Remember the first time you saw so many dolls and teddies in one place? You want to make your dolls or bears stand out from the crowd.

IDENTIFYING YOUR CREATIONS' DISTINGUISHING FEATURES

If you want your dolls and bears to be the ones collectors fall in love with, the ones they just *have* to buy, you must make them unforgettable. Go back to your research. Did you notice how many artists' dolls and bears have a signature look—something making their creations different from others? Something about your work should be distinguishable. You probably already have an idea what makes your creations different from other artists'.

Begin with what you have heard others say about your dolls and bears. If you've sold at shows, think about customers' comments. If you've been making dolls or bears for friends and family members, consider what they've said. Are your colors different and appealing? Do you make magnificent wigs? Do you make portrait dolls and include the photo in your display? Does every bear wear a smile or have eyebrows like Carol-Lynn's bears? Do you replicate costumes from historical photographs? Do you incorporate vintage fabrics in every costume? What else distinguishes your dolls and bears from those other artists are making? As we've said, there's a lot of competition out there for those discretionary dollars. If you can establish a distinguishing look, you are better able to compete. You are also better able to speak with customers at shows about your products and put together a press kit or promotional materials.

FINDING QUALITY SUPPLIES AT AFFORDABLE PRICES

The quality of your supplies is also extremely important. This doesn't mean you have to find the most expensive source for glass eyes or antique shoe buttons—only that you must find the best materials at the best prices! Occasionally, you will be willing to pay the premium prices. For instance, when you are trying a new style of mohair for teddy bears or a new source of human hair for doll wigs. If you haven't seen it in person, buy a small amount to try before you invest in a large quantity of something you may not want to use again.

When comparison shopping, look at quality and price. Ask for samples of supplies if you are buying through the mail. Sometimes it is worth it to pay a little more for something to enhance your doll or teddy bear. Stuffing is a good example. Examine different brands, qualities and types of stuffing materials. The last thing anyone wants is a lumpy doll or teddy bear. Lower-priced materials often create lumps during stuffing.

When you find materials and supplies you want to use for an edition or as a regular part of your creations, buy in volume to get maximum available discounts. If this means you'll have to live to be 150 to use them all, try networking with artists willing to make a group purchase. The less you spend on production, the higher your profits.

Doll and teddy bear artists tend to be amazing consumers of products they *have* to have. We've expanded on the old adage: The one who dies with the most fabric wins. We collect everything. This is probably addictive behavior associated with stuffing dollies and teddies. Just kidding. But we all admit to having a supply of things we'll never use! Ask other artists if they have what you're looking for. If you ask the right person, you may just find the supply that is perfect for you!

MAKING THE MOST OF YOUR SUPPLIES

Fortunately, we can utilize remnants for one-of-a-kind outfits. We've found some fantastic buys in remnant bins. Barb still has that yard of handmade imported lace that retailed for over one hundred dollars. She found it at 75 percent off! When will she use it? Who knows! But someday it will adorn a very special doll or teddy bear.

Antique dealers sometimes lower their prices during off-seasons, such as after the holidays. Vintage fabrics are always a good find. Tablecloths, bedspreads, carriage robes, and clothing are all good sources of vintage fabrics. You can use old hats to make a pattern or small hat for your doll or bear.

THE IMPORTANCE OF WORKMANSHIP

The quality of your dolls or bears is of utmost importance. Never skimp workmanship. Clip loose threads. Serge, overcast or make French seams on clothing. Use fray check on the edges of your doll bodies and teddies— especially where you close the seams after stuffing. If you make bears that wear ribbons only (rather than being fully clothed), don't skimp here. When a precious soul has only a ribbon to adorn him, it had better be a wonderful ribbon! Other teddy bears wear the artist's signature bell or beaded necklace. The smallest and least expensive touches can make a doll or teddy bear noticeable.

Quality workmanship is accomplished using quality tools. While some artists prefer to hand sew each bear or each doll costume, others machine sew. An experienced sewer will quickly tell you that newer and more expensive machines make tasks simpler. Just as the cabinetmaker uses professional-quality tools, so should you.

There's nothing more frustrating than discovering a sewing machine is creating awful loops on the underside of the fabric when the show is just hours away, or finding a seam has separated as we set up for a show—or worse, when the collector picks it up! We don't need aggravations if we can avoid them.

We're not advising you to rush out and buy the most expensive sewing machine or serger on the market today, but you should consider your equipment necessary tools of the trade. These are legitimate business expenses. Shop around. Try different brands and different models. Take scraps of materials you commonly use and sew with them. You'd probably never use materials similar to those scraps of cotton fabric stores use for demonstration purposes.

When upgrading or adding another machine, buy the best one you can afford to purchase. Ask when the model you want will go on sale. The stores know this months in advance. Go to the library. Study the yellow pages in nearby cities. Make phone calls or write for price quotes. At today's prices for machines, it can be worth a trip to another region or state to do your buying. Sales tax alone can swallow dollars.

New machines usually include free lessons. We don't buy a sewing machine as frequently as we change automobiles, yet it seems we take far less time learning to use a new sewing machine than we do learning where the controls are located in our cars! If you don't get free lessons with the machine, pay the nominal fees for the classes. You want to fully use every aspect of that new tool!

You're not being fair to yourself if you use poor-quality materials or have poor workmanship in your product. It's just as easy to do it right. If you don't know how, ask someone! Using the right tools for each task makes the work easier and gets it done faster.

LABELS, HANGTAGS AND CERTIFICATES

Are labels, hangtags and certificates necessary or important? In a word: *Yes!* Does this mean more work? Yes! However, this could be some of the most valuable work you do. Labels identify the work as yours, hangtags promote your business and offer detailed product information, and certificates enhance collectibility. Some collectors compare certificates, often preferring dolls with fancy or ornate ones. Certificates are an overlooked marketing tool! Make yours special.

LABELS

Bear artists are accustomed to putting an identifying label into the seam of each teddy bear. Teddy bears don't readily accept having information written on the back of their heads as is done with dolls. Teddy bears sold in one of the four states requiring stuffing licenses (Maine, Massachusetts, Ohio and Pennsylvania) must be identified with the corresponding stuffing license number. License application laws vary from state to state and are under the jurisdiction of the department regulating upholstery and bedding. These laws and regulations are intended to ensure and protect against fire and health hazards.

Although we've seen some artist-made teddy bears wearing several tags, each with different information, we must recommend using only one tag. Preprinted tags are available, and prices aren't staggering. Avoid companies with minimum orders of thousands of labels. Even if you have a family history of longevity, let's be reasonable. It's our dolls and teddy bears we hope will remain collectibles long after we're gone—not our supply of unused labels!

Many artists make their own labels using garment-quality leather or other sturdy nonwoven materials. Barb likes using strips of leather from light-colored old gloves. She puts her copyright mark, date and signature on the outside. If she's doing an edition exclusive to one retailer, she writes "(bear's name) for (retailer's name)" on the backside of the tag. This becomes the inside of the tag once it's folded in half and sewn into a seam. The important thing is that all pertinent information is with the bear.

Few doll artists use labels on the cloth bodies of their dolls or on the clothing. Take credit for your work. If you've created these designs, bodies and outfits, shouldn't you let people know? Also, in years to come, how will anyone know the clothing or body belongs to those doll body parts—heads, arms and legs? If you expect to be paid for your artistic endeavors, let the consumer know what you've done. Wigs, bodies and costumes are as much a part of the overall creation as the sculpted pieces, and the collector is buying your overall image.

CERTIFICATES

Certificates of Authenticity are common with artist-original dolls. Every artist should be marking the back of the doll's head with the copyright sign, date, doll's name and artist's name, and labeling the doll bodies and each article of clothing. It is also common practice to issue each doll its own certificate. Some teddy bear artists do this as well.

Certificates can be professionally printed, created on a word processor or computer, or handwritten. They should include the doll's name, edition size, number within the edition, date completed and the artist's signature. Do you have to do this? No, but it will definitely enhance your image with your collectors if you do.

HANGTAGS

Hangtags enhance your presentation and also readily identify your work as yours at shows and in shops. You can have hangtags printed and scored for folding, but this is expensive.

You can create hangtags on a computer. You can use a business card format and print them onto perforated blank papers designed for business cards. By carefully arranging the words and logo on your business cards, you can use these as folded hangtags! Tags printed horizontally can be folded in half. Punch a hole for a hangtag and you're all set. You can write information about each doll or teddy bear on the inside. Hangtags should always include your name, your business name and a contact address or telephone number. You want repeat business!

It is also possible to adapt vertically printed business cards to hangtags. Barb was forced to do this once when her hangtags were printed incorrectly and there wasn't enough time for reprinting.

Hangtags do not have to be folded. We've seen nice flat hangtags. One side has the artist's name, business name, and phone number or address. The other side has data pertaining to the specific doll or teddy bear. Barb even found some great bear-shaped card stock at a local craft shop. This would make great hangtags for teddies.

You don't have access to a computer and don't want to pay for printing? There are still alternatives. Rubber stamps are available in nearly any imaginable image. And rubber stamping is a creative world unto itself. Barb has a great rubber stamp she has yet to use! (Another one of those must-haves.) It has an oval floral design with a blank space in the middle. Barb could put the name of the doll or bear right in the middle of the oval, and all other pertinent information on the inside and back of the hangtag. Cards for rubber-stamping, and heat-activated metallic powders are also available and would make outstanding hangtags, Certificates of Authenticity or thank-you cards.

Can you use those little white string tags for price tags? Yes, if that's all you think of your work. Sound harsh? Perhaps, but why would you invest so much of yourself, your time and your money into your creations and then use a tag that makes your work look like it belongs at a flea market? You'd be much better off using hangtags to price your work. You *can* use small self-adhesive dots on your hangtags though. These can be a nice addition because the customer can remove the price without removing information you want the collector to have. This would be especially useful for dolls and teddies purchased as gifts.

Most hangtags on artist-original dolls don't have much information beside the artist's name, doll's name, edition size and the doll's number within that edition. Collectors and shop owners want to see more information: Is the wig material handmade? Glass eyes, or brand-name eyes? Was the clothing designed/made by the artist? What materials were used? Vintage fabrics? Custom-made or antique shoes? Leather shoes? You've done so much work, expended so many hours creating the entire three-dimensional picture, spent so much money for supplies; why not shout it to the world?

Hangtags should include the following information:

- The name of the teddy or doll.
- Material used to make the doll or bear, such as German mohair, English mohair, imported plush, porcelain, sculpting clay, etc.
- Type of eyes: glass, safety or antique shoe buttons for bears.
- Edition size and number of this bear or doll.

- Stuffing contents.
- Date the bear or doll was completed.
- If you have a stuffing license, you must include the number on the hangtag if your work will be sold in a state requiring a license.
- And this disclaimer: *This bear is not a toy.* Or, *This bear is not intended as a toy and may not be child safe.* Barb adds *Intended For Display Purposes ONLY.*

PRODUCT LIABILITY

You noticed those last words! Must you use them? No. Should you use them? Most definitely. Almost any doll or teddy bear could be construed as a toy by someone. And every one of us knows someone who thinks we make toys! The above disclaimer in no way protects you from lawsuits. However, it does say you are aware someone might be allergic to the fiber content, may choke on the eyes or stuffing should they become dislodged, or someone could be cut if a porcelain doll were to break.

The present laws reflect today's economic industry. Most products are produced by manufacturing facilities. Our work falls under those same laws and rules. The laws apply to manufacturers—businesses and individuals alike. Manufacturers are liable for defects in parts which they incorporate into their creations if they fail to inspect them. We don't know many artists who are experienced product or safety inspectors. In product liability suits, the plaintiff must prove injury was caused by a defect in the product and that the defect was present when the defendant had control over the item. You have absolutely no control over your creations once someone has purchased them.

There are two categories of defects: mechanical and design. Mechanical defects include loose eyes, loose screws, etc. Protect yourself by checking each piece as you make it. Pull on teddy's eyes. Does the sharp end of wire armature come close to the surface of an arm or leg? Design defects include flammability, tendency to break, toxicity and such. Most artists pay great attention to details. The majority of problems will come from using parts manufactured by someone else.

Establish your own list of test procedures, even if it's only tugging on every arm and leg, turning heads and checking eyes. Keep a record of what you include in each test and the date you conducted the test on each piece. This may sound like unnecessary paperwork, but it could save you from losing your business and even your home. Keep records of material and supply purchases. Establish a method of recording precisely what was used in each piece. You might, for example, record the product number and lot number of the mohair used when making a teddy bear.

If a collector claims she was injured because of faulty design, the burden of proof is on you. You must prove that the injury was not a result of a violation of consumer protection laws—both state and federal. This is usually very difficult to do.

Child safety laws require items to be of a certain size before the item can be recommended for young children. Size guidelines are there to prevent choking hazards. Doll's eyes fall under the list of items considered inherently dangerous. These are probably sleep eyes and this is why so many toy dollies have decals or painted eyes.

The federal agencies responsible for product liability are the Federal Trade Commission (FTC), and the Consumer Product Safety Commission (CPSC), which have offices throughout the country. They monitor the Hazardous Substance Labeling Act, the Flammable Fabrics Act, and the Consumer Product Safety Act. These laws empower the CPSC and FTC to declare any material as hazardous, to establish standards for flammability for fabrics used in clothing, household products and toys, and to regulate the composition, content and design of consumer products.

Current laws have held sellers as well as manufacturers of products liable. If a seller is held liable for a defective item, that seller may then seek reimbursement from the manufacturer through the courts. This is an instance where incorporation protects the artist. If you are incorporated, the courts can only order reimbursement from your business. However, if you are not incorporated, reimbursement may mean loss of any assets you own, including your home.

Most states have laws of strict liability by which the manufacturer can be held liable for defects that they could not have been expected to discover or prevent or even to have had knowledge of. In these instances your only protection is insurance.

The cost of liability insurance is proportional to how much business you do each year. Although rates vary from area to area, a commonly stated rate is $100 for each $10,000 of coverage. Be aware that most product liability suits result in judgments in excess of $100,000 each. Talk with your insurance agent. Compare rates and coverage offered.

We don't intend to scare you, only to inform you. Being unaware of the law is not acceptable. As believers in proactive tactics, we advise you to take time to protect yourself and your business from the hassles that easily arise from not being prepared, from failing to take the time to do what you know you should have done.

PACKAGING YOUR PRODUCT

If all your work is the same height, you may want to purchase boxes from a box manufacturer. Have them printed with your logo or name or use self-sticking labels. Some artists use tissue paper in their favorite color when packaging their dolls and teddy bears. Do this as sales increase and finances allow.

You can get as elaborate as you wish with packaging. Bear artists often use shopping bags with handles. Bears have to be able to breathe, you know. These are fine for show purchases, but not for shipping.

Make your product the best it can be! This leads to sales success.

CHAPTER FOUR

Pricing Your Dolls and Teddy Bears

*A*ll to often we hear artists saying, "Help, I don't know how to price my dolls and bears" and "I've been making bears for almost a year. Whaddaya mean I can't charge five hundred dollars?" Pricing is one of the most difficult areas for anyone working in a home-based business, especially anyone making original creations. The formula Barb has come up with is based on years in production management and cost accounting.

FINDING A COST BASE FOR EACH CREATION

First find the base cost of each doll or bear you make. This means finding and calculating the retail cost of each item used to make, finish and accessorize each item. Start with a supply of 5″×8″ index cards. Barb finds this more efficient than using a computer database because you keep the card with your creation from the moment you begin. Assign a name or a number to the doll or teddy bear, and put this at the top of the index card. Use the given name once you've decided what it will be.

To make this section easier to follow, we've made separate lists for teddy bears, porcelain dolls and one-of-a-kind direct sculpt dolls. Record each of the following items that apply to the creation of your doll or bear. Be sure to use the full retail price of each item—not the discount, wholesale, or sale price you actually paid. This will be explained in more detail later.

TEDDY BEARS
Supplies Used to Make the Bear
- Amount of fur, including the supplier, the code number (assigned by the supplier) and the retail cost of that fur
- Paw pads material
- Joints (nuts, bolts, washers, pop rivets, cotter pins)

- Spool of thread (if you didn't have the color, you'd have to buy it)
- Label
- Eyes
- Stuffing (fluff, excelsior or wood-wool, cotton, pellets)
- Armature
- Growler or squeaker
- Nose (floss, leather, suede)

Supplies Used to Finish the Bear
- Ready-made clothing (include the retail cost)
- Fabric
- Trim
- Elastic
- Buttons
- Hooks, snaps
- Appliques
- Beads, embellishments
- Shoes
- Hose, socks
- Ribbons

Accessories for Teddy Bears (If Sold With the Bear)
- Eyeglasses
- Ribbons
- Hats
- Hair ornaments
- Baskets
- Toys
- Gloves
- Jewelry
- Stand
- Chair
- Hangtags
- Certificates
- Other

If you have purchased some of these items in bulk, such as the hangtags, buttons, or labels, calculate the cost of one of these items by dividing the cost of the bulk order by the number of items in that order. For instance, if you have a bag of assorted buttons worth $20 (even if you bought them for $5), and the bag included 100 buttons, divide $20 by 100 to get $.20.

If you used five buttons on your bear's costume, you spent a total of $1 on the buttons.

Add together the costs for supplies used to make the bear. Hold onto this figure; it will stay the same, even if you choose to dress and accessorize each bear in the edition differently. To this figure, add the cost for clothing and accessories for the given bear in the edition. This is the base cost for the bear.

LIMITED-EDITION PORCELAIN OR RESIN DOLLS MADE FROM MOLDS

Basic Supplies
- One-sixth the cost of the mold (include the cost of mold release) even if the edition size is larger
- The cost of shipping (if you have your molds made for you)
- Casting material
- $10 for bisque firing
- $3 for each china paint firing (this covers the cost of paints and electricity)
- Eyes
- Wig or cost of all materials used to make wig
- Teeth

Supplies for Doll Bodies
- Armature
- Fabric
- Stuffing
- Joints
- Nylon ties, clamps
- Label

To avoid calculating this figure for each doll, if you use the same basic body construction for each doll, set a flat fee for each body size range, i.e., $10 for a doll up to 16″, $15 for a 16″ to 22″ doll, etc.

Supplies for Finishing the Doll
- Clothing (use retail cost for each of the components)
- Fabric
- Trim
- Elastic
- Buttons
- Hooks, snaps

"String-a-long" Bear (One of a Kind)

Description	List	Actual
1/3 yd XYZ string mohair dye lot #123 from Co. A	63.00	50.40
12mm glass eyes from Company B	3.60	2.80
Black pearl Cotton #5 for nose + mouth	1.85	1.30
4 gray upholstery fabric paw pads	3.00 S+H 1.00	S+H 1.00
Stone Stuffing 26 oz @ 2.35.06	364	364 ★
Authentic Model Eq Register w/ case #N012B	35.00	13.00
2 set miniature coins from tate Website Co.	8.00	6.40
3/4 yd neck ribbon #9876 from ABC Ribbon Co.	1.42	1.42
	120.51	80.96
label	.05	.05
	120.56	81.01

Q * by price would indicate the item is probably not available or not at that price. An example would be a "find" at an antique shop.

Sample index card for a bear

- Appliques
- Beads, embellishments
- Shoes
- Hose, socks

Accessories for Dolls (If Sold With the Doll)
- Hats
- Hair ornaments
- Baskets
- Toys
- Gloves
- Jewelry
- Eyeglasses
- Stand
- Chair
- Hangtags
- Certificates

Add these costs together. This is your cost base for each doll in the edition.

POLYMER AND SOFT-SCULPTED DOLLS
Basic Supplies for Polymer and Soft-Sculpted Dolls
- Sculpting material
- Armature for heads
- Eyes
- $3 for each time you cure the body parts
- Wig or cost of all materials used to make the wig
- $5 for paints
- Flosses and paints used for soft sculpted faces

Supplies for Doll Bodies
- Armature
- Fabric
- Stuffing
- Joints
- Nylon ties, clamps
- Label
- Other

Set a flat fee for each body size range, i.e., $10 for dolls up to 16″, $15 for 16″ to 22″ dolls, and so on.

Card #183

"Brittni" Porcelain edition of 15 - portrait doll

Description	Est.	Actual
25 lbs T-10 groggy earth clay for original sculpture .15	1.07	.76
1/6th cost of 25 lbs mold plaster for waste mold	2.94	2.94
1/6th cost of 24 lbs mold plaster for working mold	2.53	2.53
1/6th cost of porcelain for 2 waste castings	1.17	1.17
1/6th cost of mold release for 2 mold sets	.38	.38
1/3 gal of porcelain slip	4.70	4.23
1/6 gal firing of rough pour	1.67	1.67
1/6 res. pour firing of waste pour	.50	.50
Soft firing of finished piece	3.00	3.00
Bisque firing of finished piece	10.00	10.00
6 China paint firings @ $3.00 each	18.00	18.00
(Even if you fire several dolls at once !!)	—	
Body part Base price	45.96	45.18

Sample index cards for a porcelain or resin doll (cont. through page 31)

Buttini card #293 Assembly costs

	Est.	Actual
20mm Noyes Real Eyes	13.10	7.88
Klobal human hair wig	35.00	21.01
Hand made teeth	3.00	1.00
Neck/shoulder assembly for connection	9.50	3.70
6 ft electrical wire 10/3 flat for armature	17.52	15.12
3/4 yd body fabric	4.50	3.38
4.5 lbs Stone Buffing	9.00	9.00
Waxed linen to secure limbs to body	1.35	1.35
Label	.05	.05
Twill tape to secure shoulder plate to body	1.55	1.20
Base price of body (assembly costs)	82.82	63.69

Britton Card #3 of 3	List	Actual
3 yd imported floral faux Andrew	54.00	42.50
6 yd antique hand crocheted lace	18.06	9.00*
2 yd bottle for slip + pantaloons	30.00	28.00
1 yd elastic	.65	.65
4 Buttons	2.00	1.50
1 thread	2.29	1.89
Shoes - pink patent leather	16.99	8.99
Pearl earring + necklace	20.00	14.00
Storybook	5.00	5.00
Finishing Costs	164.93	111.53
Bear Price	45.96	45.18
Assembly Price	82.82	63.65
Add Actual costs of doll only	297.71	220.46

(No costs of doing business or packaging are included.)

Supplies for Finishing the Doll
- Ready-made clothing
- Fabric
- Trim
- Elastic
- Buttons
- Hooks, snaps
- Appliques
- Beads, embellishments
- Shoes
- Hose, socks
- Other

Accessories for Dolls (If Sold With the Doll)
- Hats
- Hair ornaments
- Baskets
- Toys
- Gloves
- Jewelry
- Eyeglasses
- Stand
- Chair
- Hangtags
- Certificates
- Other

Add all these costs. This is the cost base for the doll.

When you begin selling your dolls and bears, you won't have expense figures for the previous year's costs of doing business. Therefore, you can only use the cost base above as the basis for your pricing formula. Your minimum wholesale price for the doll or bear is three times the cost base. Your minimum retail price is five times the cost base. These are minimums. If you price your work lower than this, you will probably lose money, and your dolls or bears will appear suspiciously underpriced. Collectors will think this reflects their quality.

ADDING IN YOUR BUSINESS COSTS

If you have been in business at least a year, look back at your Schedule C from last year's taxes to determine about how much you spent to keep

	List	Actual
"Jarrell" one-of-a-kind cernit doll		
2 pkg caramel cernit	29.00	14.00
16 mm Real eyes	9.80	5.88
Head armature	1.00	1.00
3 ft electrical wire for armature	3.87	3.87
4 "firings" @ $3 each	12.00	12.00
Paints	5.00	5.00
Mohair wig - hand made by artist	45.00	25.00
Base Price	105.67	69.75
Body for 23" doll - pre established costs	15.00	15.00
Vintage dress fabric used for outfit	18.00	18.00
Thread	2.29	1.89
Undies fabric	6.00	7.00
Outfit soy & shoes	40.00	28.00
Teddy bear - artist original	68.00	40.00
Total	326.71	179.64

Odd →

Sample index card for a one-of-a-kind polymer clay doll

your business running. To review, the following items should be included in this figure:

- Cost of film, film processing, or professional photos of your bears or dolls. One-quarter the cost of a camera or special lenses you purchased in order to do your own photography.
- Actual costs for business cards, letterheads, envelopes, rubber stamps, printed forms, flyers, brochures and postage used in one year. If you have five hundred forms printed but only use one hundred, compute the cost for one hundred.
- Business card holder, table covers, shelving, risers, display items, decorations for booth display, lighting and light bulbs used while attending shows.
- Booth/table rental, including any added charges for electrical services, additional tables, etc.
- Telephone calls made for business purposes.
- One-fifth the cost of a computer, printer, fax machine or word processor purchased for your business.
- Magazine subscriptions, books, and other publications related to your business.
- The number of miles you drove for business purposes multiplied by $.35 for your annual vehicle expenses.
- Advertising expenses.
- Business-related legal or accounting fees.
- Dues to professional organizations.
- Any other business-related expenses.

Add these figures. This is your total cost of doing business. If you anticipate doing more shows this year, spending more on advertising, or driving more miles, try to figure this into your business expenses. Of course, this amount will not be perfect, but a ballpark figure will work.

Divide this figure by the number of dolls or bears you anticipate offering for sale in the coming year. If you intend to complete less than twenty-five items, use the number 25. This will give you your cost of doing business for each doll or bear. Add this number to the base cost of each bear and doll which you figured earlier, and use this final number to calculate your wholesale and retail price for that doll or bear.

For example:

Base cost of bear: $50
Total Business Expenses: $6,000

Number of bears offered for sale: 100
$6,000 divided by 100 = $60
$50 + $60 = $110
Minimum wholesale price of this bear: $110 × 3 = $330
Minimum retail price of this bear: $110 × 5 = $550

Obviously, the more experience you have, the more money you will be willing, and able, to spend up front. Usually your demand will increase, but so will your business costs. If you continue to include your business costs in the price of your bears or dolls, your business will remain profitable. The consumer will see your raised prices as an indication of your experience and the demand for your work. Newer doll and teddy bear artists do not have this luxury. Collectors know they are new on the scene, even if the quality of their creations is just as good as those of the well-known artist.

WHAT ABOUT THE TIME I SPEND PRODUCING?

Artists ask, "When can I start adding in the cost of my time?" Many artists do set an hourly wage for themselves, keep records on how much time they put into each piece, and include this in the cost of the doll or bear. Barb has an unconventional approach to this. She has extensive experience in commercial production that is not doll- and bear-related. She prefers to include the retail cost of each supply when figuring the base cost of each doll. Because she is buying supplies at wholesale or discount prices, the difference pays for the time she spends making and selling her dolls and teddy bears.

Over the years Barb has found that using this method is easier than keeping track of her hours, and the resulting cost is similar. The time it takes to make the first of a new design varies greatly from the time it takes to do the final doll or bear in an edition. The time spent making one-of-a-kind dolls or bears varies considerably, even if each is equal in quality. While she could average the time spent on a doll or bear and use this average number of hours as a cost to include in the base cost for each, using the retail price of the supplies is more consistent.

Pricing your dolls and bears will take some getting used to. You may have to make some adjustments along the way. Eventually you will become comfortable keeping track of costs, and will find the prices that best fit your market and encourage rather than inhibit sales.

PART TWO

Marketing Yourself and Your Business

CHAPTER FIVE

Marketing Yourself Along With Your Dolls and Bears

*M*any people are offering dolls and teddy bears for sale— all to the same limited number of buyers. Remember, discretionary funds (mad money) are scarce now. Maybe your favorite collector has decided to move on to collecting hubcaps. Or (horrors!) maybe she has had enough of your designs and is buying Sally Smith's.

How do you make your dolls and teddy bears more desirable than your competitors'? (In this marketplace jungle, all your friendly colleagues are also your competitors.) Someone once said, "There's a fool for every product." There's a buyer somewhere for everything (remember pet rocks?). There's room for you. To find your place in the jungle, learn to market wisely.

Marketing means taking aggressive steps to promote your product. But successful marketing also means promoting an image of yourself *and* your business. Danny Mac, a professional sales trainer who presents some of today's best sales seminars, will tell you there are only four reasons why a customer doesn't make a purchase: you, your product, your company and your price. Notice that *you* are listed first. You are the most important part of this sales philosophy. Unknown artists aren't necessarily making dolls or teddy bears any less wonderful than the well-known artists' pieces. The well-known artists are simply better at marketing.

You must make your persona something perfect strangers will want to buy into. Today, collectors of artist-made original dolls and teddy bears are buying not only the art object but a part of the soul of its artist/ designer. We refer to this as the *mystique surrounding success*. It's always around successful people. Lee Iacocca was the persona behind the Chrysler Corporation. Bill Gates *is* Microsoft. Let's learn how to make *you* into a best-selling product.

THE CONSTANT ELEMENT IN
YOUR BUSINESS—YOU!

Your dolls and bears will evolve as you make each one. You will try different sizes, styles, themes, mediums or types of fur. Your most recent doll or teddy bear may look nothing like your first. Yet, as your creations change, one thing remains constant—*you!* You are the creator behind each piece, and each carries a small part of you within.

If you have read chapter 4, you have already considered what makes your creations special. You have probably not considered how important your own image or persona is to your sales. Throughout your career as a doll or teddy bear artist, your height will remain the same, although your weight and hair color may change. Your clothing style may change, but your voice will still be recognized. You probably will not change your name other than by marriage, and today many women choose to retain their maiden names. Your name is a part of what is constant and central to marketing—*you.*

Think of the lovely restaurant you always stop at for lunch when you travel to a certain locale. The decor may change, the menu may change— the name may even change—but there's something that draws you back. It may be the view, the ambience, the excellent service, the personal touch of the owners. This is the constant within that restaurant.

Likewise, your persona is the constant in your dolls and teddy bears. You are your product and your product is you. Wherever you go, you are an ambassador for your work and your business.

If you don't believe that your persona makes a difference, consider this story. The promoter of a large California show recently received a phone call from a woman who had attended the show. She pleaded with the promoter for help. She had purchased a doll and wanted another, but she couldn't remember the vendor's name or booth. She did remember what the woman looked like and what she was wearing. Her description of the vendor was so accurate the promoter knew exactly who the woman was trying to reach—even though this was the first time this vendor had exhibited at the promoter's show! *Image. Persona.* The vendor was remembered not by what she was selling, but by the image she projected. She successfully marketed herself.

EVALUATING YOUR LOOK

Consider your look. Do not overlook this vital step. Make the investment in time and money for a cosmetics and hair makeover. Have your colors done. Find a salon offering programs showing you how to choose the most flattering clothing styles for your body shape. If your body isn't in its best shape, take steps to fix it. You'll be amazed at how much better you will feel about yourself.

Imagine the time you'll save shopping for clothes when you look only at outfits in your colors. Or at styles best for your body shape. No more wasted hours trying on clothes in a dressing room only to go home empty-handed—or worse yet, with something you don't like and that will not be flattering on you. Knowing what works best leaves time for important things—like creating your treasures! Tell yourself it's an investment.

Whenever you're meeting collectors and shop owners, you must shine. This is *not* the time to camouflage yourself. Do you wear dark or muted colors to these events? Do you hide behind that favorite hat, telling yourself it's artistic? Or worse, that it's your *signature* look? Remember, few can carry this off, and it's usually *after* they have attained a level of success.

Go through your closets. Inspect your wardrobe. Set aside outfits that show you off. If they aren't there, go shopping. You do not have to invest heavily in a new wardrobe. Discount shopping areas dot our countryside. If you've had your colors done and really listened to the explanations of which styles look best on you, this won't be a major undertaking.

Think of the reaction your display will get at shows when you incorporate these lessons into your presentation, or when costuming your dolls and teddy bears. When the collector or shop owner is shopping for new dolls and bears, there are many from which to choose. The smallest detail can make the difference between your creation and the one in the next booth. If your work is presented in the best possible way, the customer is more likely to select your doll or teddy. Learn which colors work best together. Learn which do *not* work well. Don't display the wrong colors next to one another.

You say you couldn't begin to understand this process? Almost every one of us who dresses our bears or who makes dolls (we don't know anyone who sells naked dolls!) spends time draping different colors and patterns over finished dolls and bears trying to decide which is best. If you have a video camera, now is the time to use it. See your work as others will. This will help you objectively look at your presentation and improve it to attract more buyers. Just as proper lighting, pleasant aromas and embers glowing in a fireplace enhance the home during an open house and make it more attractive to prospective buyers, an inviting personal appearance makes you seem more approachable to buyers and collectors.

Finally, don't forget about footwear. You will need comfortable shoes for shows. You will be standing and standing and standing. Keep your shoes comfortable but not attention-getting. (Don't wear those comfortable well-worn walking shoes, please.) Make sure your footwear is cleaned and polished. You would be amazed at how many people *look* at what others have on their feet. Everything you wear sends messages about how you perceive yourself.

OVERCOMING SHYNESS

How do people perceive your body language? What messages are you sending to your collectors? Go back to the research you did after reading chapter 1. What made the successful artists appear successful at shows?

At a recent show, an artist Barb knows appeared standoffish because her body language was abrupt. Artists and collectors wondered why she seemed so unapproachable. This was not the way they expected her to act. The following week Barb spoke with her about this problem. She was unaware that she had presented such an unpleasant image and was glad that Barb had told her. At her next show a few weeks later, she was well received. What had changed? Her attention to herself and her persona!

Creative people are often an insecure bunch. We sometimes prefer to place a buffer or safety zone between ourselves and collectors. We build a shield protecting our vulnerability—or so we tell ourselves. What do you do at shows? Are you behind your booth working on your next teddy bear or sketching a costume design with the belief you're letting the collectors see you create? These are all defense mechanisms—tools you're using to shield yourself from people with spending money in their pockets. These people should be buying your dolls and bears!

If you are shy or have a difficult time greeting customers, or if you just find many customers uninterested in your dolls or bears because your products are high end and appeal only to a few, whatever the reason, you're making an excuse. Excuses are negatives. Change that negative into a positive. Get out of your hiding place. Push your table to the back of your booth space. You can move your table at most shows so it is at the rear of your area. *You* stand in front of the table. Do whatever it takes to rearrange your display so you cannot retreat behind it.

You're out in the open, right there in front of everything. People are coming to your booth or table. Talk with them! These are your potential customers! Don't stand silently by as they admire a doll or teddy bear. Tell them about that doll! How else is anyone to know you made her wig? Or her clothing is made from vintage fabric you discovered when on vacation in a quaint New England town? Tell them about that teddy bear! Does he have antique shoe button eyes? What kind of mohair did you use? Talk about your work. Ask how they see your doll or teddy bear in their collection!

Remember the old saying, you never get a second chance to make a first impression. Sell yourself. Watch your sales improve.

CHAPTER SIX

Build Name Recognition

The first step in promoting yourself is establishing name recognition. Every successful artist (those with names you recognize) has worked very hard to earn that name recognition. It doesn't just happen. And we don't know any doll or teddy bear artist who uses a public relations professional to get name recognition.

In chapters following this, we will show you how to gain free publicity from the press, photograph your creations for publicity purposes, and make decisions related to advertising. In this chapter, we will explain the best ways to use your involvement in the doll and teddy bear industries to gain name recognition.

ESTABLISHING LOCAL RECOGNITION

Start locally. Name recognition in your own city, town or area will go a long way. It took quite a while to select the right business card. Use it. Everyone you meet should know what you do. Everyone. Your banker (the manager, assistant manager, and every teller), your hair stylist, your pharmacist, the dry cleaner, automobile service technician, your insurance agent, store salespersons wherever you do business. You didn't have business cards printed so they could sit in your desk drawer. One advantage to having a name almost no one can spell correctly is that it gives Barb and Carol-Lynn an excuse to pass out business cards!

It may feel odd at first to pass your business card to everyone you meet. But this method has brought many customers our way—buying customers, repeat customers, serious customers. Your automobile service technician may not want to buy a doll or teddy bear for himself, but perhaps he wants to get his daughter started collecting something of value, or maybe his wife or mother-in-law loves dolls or teddies and is looking for additions to her collection. You never know when a contact could be lucrative.

LECTURES AND PROGRAMS

One of the best ways to gain name recognition and educate the public about your craft at the same time is by presenting educational programs. Anyone can do this. Barb was among the shyest of the shy in high school. She would rather have had the building cave in on her than to get in front of a class for any kind of presentation! By graduate school, she had learned to mentally prepare herself for something she did not want to do, realizing that it only consumed a small block of time. Now, several lifetimes later, she's comfortable before any number of people.

What's changed besides age and experience? We are confident when we speak with knowledge and experience. We believe in our convictions. What we say and do comes from within each of us just like our creativity. Believing in oneself is the secret to successful public speaking and presentations. If you can talk to one person, you can speak to many at one time.

There are numerous opportunities to lecture about your work, about collecting, about the history of dolls or bears, or any other personal area of expertise. Do whatever you know best. Barb has managed to present programs to several different audiences. If she can do it, you can too. After all, no one knows your work as well as you do.

Begin at your local library. Barb's local library asked her to do a presentation on anything she wanted related to her dolls. She prepared a program that gently explained the difference between the artist-made originals and manufactured and hobbyist-made dolls. In it she demonstrated the process of making a porcelain doll, from the original clay sculpture through the mold-making process, to finishing the doll and sculpting one-of-a-kind polymer clay dolls. Barb didn't expect much of a turnout. She expected no more than fifteen people and hoped there would be at least five. Was she ever surprised! Over one hundred people came for the first presentation. The library staff had to turn away nearly forty more.

This led to a televised interview on the local public-access cable channel. This show was taped and was rebroadcast over one hundred times in two years. Barb has given the same presentation (modified slightly to suit the audience) over fifty times to various civic and professional groups, nursing homes, schools and clubs.

There is no greater joy than seeing the light of understanding in the eyes of the people attending these presentations. All of a sudden they realize that an artist can't possibly produce many hundreds or thousands of any one doll or teddy bear without some help—and that usually means a manufacturer. Educating the public about the differences between artist-made and artist-designed pieces will enhance appreciation of your work.

People want to learn about what they collect and about what they are spending their money on. An added bonus is that you will need to bring samples of your work with you to demonstrate these concepts. These examples will change as the dolls and teddies are sold and new ones are added. Soon you will have people attending your presentations just to see your latest work! And, many buy! Presentations are like a one-person show.

It's a good idea to videotape your presentations. If you do not own a video camera, rent one. It will prove a marvelous tool. You will be too busy giving your presentation to worry about the camera. Review the tape soon after the presentation. Watch yourself. Listen to what you said. Critique yourself. Learn what you are doing right. Find those little things you want to eliminate from your next presentation.

There is a wonderful added benefit to doing presentations for libraries, museums, schools, clubs and civic groups. These groups publicize their presentations. They publish this information in their newsletters. Those groups sponsoring presentations open to the public also send press releases to local media. This is free publicity for you and your work!

TAILORING YOUR PRESENTATION TO YOUR AUDIENCE

One of the most humorous statements in Barb's presentations has always been, "Doll and teddy bear artists don't clean house and we don't cook—it's a rule." She had to drop that line when the majority of the audience arrived by a chauffeur-driven automobile to one of her lectures! They would not understand cleaning the house or cooking the way the typical audience would.

Once you've chosen a subject for a presentation, you can "recycle" the same information in different formats depending on your audience. The most difficult presentation Barb ever gave was to a double-period class of high school freshmen at the high school she had attended. All sorts of horrifying thoughts ran through her head as she drove the ten miles to the school. *What are you thinking?* she asked herself. She was going to tell a room full of fourteen- and fifteen-year-olds she'd given up a career in engineering and management consulting to make dollies. Yeah, right. Those kids had no choice about attending the presentation. They had to be in the classroom. And to top it all off, the classroom was right across the hall from where Barb's least favorite class had been.

As you can probably tell, Barb was not in the best frame of mind at this point. But the talk went remarkably well. Barb did change her prepared presentation. Good thing she had long ago learned to adjust to her audience. She focused on the fact that these young people were just about to embark on their adult lives, and that the day-to-day responsibilities could easily consume their time and energies. She told them they needed to learn to take time out of their busy weeks to create something—something they could later look back on and say, "I did that." We all need to have something to make us feel good about ourselves when we have "one of those days."

Did they understand? During the ninety-minute presentation, Barb passed around several balls of Cernit, a polymer sculpting clay. This is not something she usually includes as part of a presentation, but she wanted those students to see how it felt to create something of their own. Again, Barb was adjusting her presentation to the audience. One young man in the room created a face. He crumpled that up and then created a perfect hand holding a ball. Hands are the most difficult part of a doll for many artists to sculpt. This is probably because we cannot keep our own hands posed as a model while we sculpt. That young man has since completed an apprentice course with Barb. His first sculpture was a wonderful rendition of a basketball player!

WORKSHOPS AND CLASSES

Teaching is a great way to build clientele—and name recognition. Each time you teach a workshop at a show, your name appears in the show program and local media. Collectors jump at the chance to get close to their favorite artist. Many are dying to try their hands at making a doll or bear! Tailor your presentation to your audience.

Each of us can learn something from another person. Even experienced artists can discover there's a tool they've never thought of using. Common screwdrivers can be modified to bend cotter pins. Dowels are stuffing tools. A dog grooming brush is an essential tool for every bear artist. Babs Murdock makes magnificent miniature teddies. She didn't know what she was supposed to use for eyes, but she discovered small brads in the hardware store that worked perfectly for her. These discoveries didn't find their way into the mainstream doll or teddy bear industry without workshops or classes. Of course, this probably happened after some very frustrating experiences were viewed by logical problem-solving minds!

A few artists fear sharing their secrets with others. Don't let insecurities stifle your career. Creative work comes from within. No one ever lost creative talent by sharing it with another.

Workshops and classes have always financially helped artists. The artist is paid for the presentation, and the participants commonly buy a doll or bear from the artist. At the very least, students will talk to their friends about the workshop and the artist. And this builds name recognition.

PUBLIC DISPLAYS

How often have you noticed artwork displayed in enclosed, protected kiosks or windows in banks, libraries, malls, stores, lobbies of office buildings? Many times there is no charge for this space. This is another opportunity for you to educate others about your craft and publicize your work as well.

An educational display is appropriate for libraries, museums and schools. Show something about how your dolls and teddies are made. Armatures, joints, stuffing, and raw materials can be displayed with the finished pieces. Of course, you would include your name and phone number with the display. Remember to give a supply of personal data sheets about yourself to a receptionist or other person working near the display. People will ask for information about the artist.

ENTERING CONTESTS

Entering your work into competitions enhances your name recognition. We must admit, neither of us does this, but it does work. Many shows include some sort of competition. The public looks at these pieces and at the names of those who created each piece. This helps collectors associate your name with your style.

Dolls—The Collector's Magazine, Doll Reader, Teddy Bear Review and *Teddy Bear & Friends* each have contests. Finalists are announced in the magazine and the public votes for favorites in a variety of categories. Being nominated for one of these awards is invaluable for getting and maintaining name recognition. The dolls and teddy bears receiving the nominations are pictured in the magazines, and the artists' names are published and posted in numerous places.

If you think you wouldn't stand a chance, think again. Only days prior to the deadline for the 1996 *Dolls* Award of Excellence, Barb encouraged (pushed is a more accurate word) a friend to enter at least one of her dolls. She entered two, a vinyl doll and a resin doll. Each doll received a nomination in its category.

If you do enter these contests, follow through. The nominees for at least one of the contests are selected by a panel of shop owners. Don't assume your work will stand out from the rest. The selection process is exhausting, especially if it's done at the International Toy Fair. How can you stand out in the crowd? The judges are shop owners, and their names are not kept secret. Check *The Teddy Bear Sourcebook* and *The Doll Sourcebook* for the address of their shop. If they advertise, check magazines. Send photos of your entries along with an information sheet about you and your entries to each judge beforehand. But please don't say you entered these dolls or teddy bears for awards! Simply send the information as you would to any other shop owner whom you would like to interest in ordering your work. See chapter 11 for more advice on sending mass mailings to retailers.

Nominees' names are published numerous times. Some artists will tell you that being nominated brought more name recognition than winning the actual award!

AUCTION DONATIONS

We know, we know. Everyone wants a donation. However, if you make your selections carefully, auction donations can be a beneficial tool. Look for auctions that are well publicized and well attended. If you are not knowledgeable about how the auction is conducted, attend the auction before making a donation.

If you have the opportunity to set a minimum bid amount, be sure to do so. Understand that the right collectors might not be there and you don't want to give your work away. It does not enhance you, your work or that of any other doll or teddy bear artist if your work is sold for far less than its real value. In fact, you want your piece to sell at auction for far more than you'd ever achieve on your own.

Art organizations usually want an annual donation. This donation should be a tool for you as well. We each donate regularly to certain educational scholarship auctions. We have both cultivated quite a list of regular bidders who are now regular customers. This probably would not have happened if we did not donate to these auctions.

Every state has public broadcast television stations. Each of these holds an annual auction. Investigate their advertising and promotional techniques for artwork. Will they include your work with other artist-created pieces? You don't want to be included with the toys—your work is too collectible and expensive! These auctions, if well done, can give you wide exposure.

JOINING ORGANIZATIONS

The more people you know, the better your sales become. Juried artist organizations are a good choice. The networking and professional guidance from other artists is priceless. Your membership in juried artist organizations will enhance your name recognition. Organizations for both artists and collectors put you in touch with collectors who might love your work. This enhances your name recognition and sales. For a long list of doll and teddy bear organizations and contact people, see *The Doll Sourcebook* and *The Teddy Bear Sourcebook*.

Get involved in organizations that have nothing to do with dolls or bears. You don't have to commit all your time to these groups, but they are wonderful places to make contacts. Spending a few hours a month doing something different refreshes your mind and creativity, too.

These organizations can enhance skills that will help your sales. If you are hesitant about public speaking, consider the Toastmasters club in your area. Membership in business organizations can greatly enhance your business skills. You will learn what has worked for other small business owners. Every business started small!

WRITING OPPORTUNITIES

If you can speak, you can write. Everyone deals with verbal communication on a daily basis. The most engrossing written material is written as if the writer were speaking with you.

Where do you begin? Write about what you do, where you've been, your newest creations. Chapter 8 will give you more information about writing and distributing press releases about your work. But don't stop there. Write to doll and teddy bear magazines and ask for their submission guidelines. Do you have a great idea for a story? Even if it is not about yourself or your work, your name and biography will appear with the story and build your name recognition.

Submit articles with photos to several sources. Many local newspapers also accept freelance submissions. Any writing you do about dolls or bears will benefit you and build name recognition. Do you know of a local collector with a magnificent collection? The feature editor of your local paper would probably love an article about her!

The more often collectors see and hear your name—even if it is not directly connected to your work—the better off you'll be. Remember, you're marketing yourself as well as your creations!

CHAPTER SEVEN

Photographing Your Dolls and Bears

*A*ny design-centered business depends on its image. The doll and teddy bear worlds are no exception. As artists and designers our biggest selling point is the originality and uniqueness of our product. We're lucky. Our product, if we present it in the proper light, will speak for itself. Chapters 8 and 10 will cover strategies for getting free publicity from the press and for spending advertising dollars. But before you can do this you need good "selling" photographs of your work.

In many ways, our customers are addicts. They page through collector magazines and books looking for the perfect face, the one that speaks to something inside them and makes them feel safe and loved. Not every collector will have the chance to see your creations in person. You want to reach a collector base far larger than collectors who see your work at shows or in shops.

To sell to them you need to capture the spirit of your doll or bear on film. Then you need to get your photos out there: to editors, writers, shops and enthusiasts. A great photo of your work can inspire orders and offers from people and places half a world away.

WHY DO IT YOURSELF?

We're asking the photographs to do the near impossible. We're asking them to make viewers believe our inanimate brainchildren have a life, a soul, a personality. Through art and artiface, through the means of light and shadow transferred to paper, we must capture the far-flung customer's heart and purse and keep him coming back for more.

You can do it. Maybe your first efforts won't be prize-winners. But you have an advantage over the professional photographer down the block. You know your work intimately. And you have an artistic eye. No one else can see your work as you do, nor can they present it to the public as you envision it.

Photographing dolls and bears requires the combined skills of still life, portrait, commercial and art photography. Any professional photographer you may hire will not only be expensive, but probably will not be competent in all these areas. Chances are, she will not be able to capture the personality of your creations. To you, they're alive. To her, they're still life.

Psychologists giving tests for determining suitability for professions report only 5 percent of the population is creative. You have an advantage over 95 percent of the population: an artist's eye. Put your creativity, and your special way of seeing to work behind the viewfinder. You'll be able to present your product in an artful "signature" style and inspire other signatures on the "dotted line."

If you photograph your dolls, you won't worry about infringing someone else's copyright or getting permission to use the shots. You own the negatives. You can do whatever you want with your photos—print them any which way, use them for promotion, put them onto CD-ROM discs. Your name will be on the photo credit line: an effective subliminal sales tool.

You say you haven't the patience to learn to photograph your work?

Maybe not with the kids, housework or your mother-in-law. But you do have it in abundance. Patience gives you the ability to zero in on your art, to get lost in it all night, thinking you'd been at it only an hour. All artists know this feeling, this experience. Maybe it's not patience. Maybe it's aesthetic obsession. In this alternate reality, problems aren't work. They're a challenge, a key to being able to do the part of the project that's fun. You've been in this space. That's where photography lives. Go visit. You'll feel at home.

TOOLS OF THE TRADE

As with any art form, the tools you use in photography affect the final outcome of the project. To take publishable photos, you need the following equipment:

- An adjustable camera (preferably non-automatic, with optional lenses)
- Film
- A light source
- An undistracted place to take photos

- A "seamless backdrop"
- A tripod
- A light meter
- Patience
- An "artistic eye"

Please, don't empty your bank account to finance your photo studio. Before you buy out the local photo shop, see what you can do with what you already own. Maybe there's a photo shop from which you can rent equipment or purchase used equipment. If you can afford only one item, make it a good non-automatic 35mm single lens reflex camera. It will pay for itself.

TYPES OF CAMERAS

Nearly any camera from the five-and-dime point-and-shoot to the professional caliber $8'' \times 10''$ view camera, can be used to take photos of bears and dolls. If you have a good eye, a lot of patience and some luck, you'll take good photos with a point-and-shoot. But, because it's an automatic camera, you won't have any control over important functions like shutter speed or depth of field.

Even if your point-and-shoot is a 35mm camera, it's still not a great choice for doll and bear photography. The 35mm point-and-shoot cameras are in the Rangefinder family. Rangefinder cameras are made so the viewfinder and lens are slightly offset. What you see in the viewfinder is not exactly what the lens sees. This is why, even though you *know* you've perfectly framed your shots, they come back from the processor with legs or heads missing. This phenomenon is called parallax error, and some pretty expensive 35mm cameras produce it.

One type of 35mm camera does not. It is called a Single Lens Reflex (SLR). It is made so the viewfinder looks through the lens, allowing you to see exactly what the lens sees. SLRs can see a wider variety of objects and perspectives than Rangefinder cameras, no matter how automatic, because they can be equipped with a vast wardrobe of lenses, from telephoto (for seeing distance) to macro (for seeing tiny things). This is the camera Carol-Lynn and Barb use and recommend you use, to photograph dolls and bears.

SLR cameras come in many sizes and styles, from totally manual to totally automatic. Some *beep* when the camera is in focus. Others automatically bracket shots. In one line of SLRs, you can "dial" your eyesight into the camera's viewing system. As you move your eye across the viewfinder and focus on objects, the camera duplicates your focus. Carol-Lynn has one of these cameras and it's a blessing as her eyesight deteriorates (too many hours spent making bears, no doubt.)

You don't need any fancy features. For years, Carol-Lynn took award-winning photos of dolls and bears, published in magazines, books and newspapers, and as magazine covers with the most basic Pentax brand SLR, which cost about $150. Her only addition to the standard equipment was a 100mm portrait lens with macro capabilities, allowing her to focus on small objects. This cost about $100.

Whatever camera you choose, get intimately acquainted with it. You will be having a long, profitable relationship. Read your manual and try everything in it. Learn what your camera can and cannot do. Read photo books and magazines for new ideas and techniques to use.

If you need help learning about your camera, try the following:

• Join your local camera club. Ask a camera shop about clubs in your area. Someone in the club is bound to know about cameras like yours. Participate in club activities. You'll learn the ins and outs of your camera by using it. Most camera club activities include model shoots, field trips, expeditions, competitions, participation in conferences and conventions. Best of all, you'll have people in the club with whom you can "talk photography." You will also be making contacts in the community that may eventually lead to sales of your dolls or bears.

• Take a photography class. You can find classes offered through your local technical school, adult education classes, colleges or junior colleges in your area. You may be able to audit a college class. Take a photo workshop. These are advertised in photography magazines, and are available for photographers at any level. Carol-Lynn has taken many of these, each focusing on one aspect of photography, like "on location lighting for portraiture."

• Ask for help at a local full-service camera shop. Some photo shops run workshops and festivals featuring representatives from camera manufacturers. Not only do they give presentations and tips, but sometimes they sell accessories like lenses at the store's cost.

• Visit camera expositions. Look in the paper of the nearest large city for announcements of camera shows: expositions featuring all the latest equipment from photographic manufacturers. Representatives from the manufacturer of your camera may be able to help you if you catch them at a good time.

LENSES

Most SLR cameras come with a 55mm lens if you buy "off the shelf." 55mm or 50mm is so commonly used it's called a *normal lens.* Who wants normal? We're artist photographers. When buying a camera, purchase body and lens separately. Choose a 90mm or 100mm lens, one with optional macro capability, if possible. This will let you focus on small things like eyes, nose, embroidery, details of clothing, or miniature bears or dolls.

Professional portrait photographers choose a 90mm to 100mm lens because of how it "sees" the model. Look through one. You'll see differently.

If you only have a normal lens, don't toss your camera. You can and will make good, "selling" photos with it. It's the photographer's *eye,* not her lens, that counts.

FILM

Most magazine and book editors, until recently, preferred either black-and-white 8" × 10" glossy prints or 35mm Kodachrome slides.

Color prints were looked upon as amateur. Until recently it was difficult to get good, crisp, true prints in a publication using color print originals. This is changing with the advent of computerized scanning and printing and the option of storing photos on computer discs. The variety and quality of professional quality color film is expanding. Some publishers are actually asking for color prints.

Don't ignore the industry standard. If you shoot black-and-white and/or color slide (transparency) film, editors and ad departments will thank you and think you're a pro.

Each type of film comes in many speeds. These are indicated by a number preceded with the letters ASA or ISO. The higher the ASA or ISO number, the faster the speed.

The faster the speed, the more grain a film has. Grain is the term used for the annoying (sometimes "artistic") spots that make some color photos look like Impressionist paintings and some black-and-white prints look like comic strip panels. Unless you are deliberately looking for an arty, soft, grainy look, choose the slowest film you can easily handle, preferably ASA 100 film, which is available in black and white or color.

Color print film has the word *color* in its brand name: Fujicolor, Kodacolor. All use the same chemical processes for developing.

Color slide film has *chrome* in its name: Fujichrome, Ektachrome, Kodachrome. Kodachrome (ASA 64) has long enjoyed popularity in the publishing world. Kodachrome film can be processed only by a Kodak lab. This usually involves mailing your film to another location. If you are in a time crunch, this can cause problems. Standard color print and slide films can be processed almost anywhere. But you'll have to search around for a lab to do your black and white.

Each manufacturer's color film has a personality to its color balance. Some are greener, some are bluer. Most amateur color print film seems rather vivid. Try a variety; see which has the color balance to best represent your work.

Two types of film are generally available: amateur and professional.

Amateur film is widely available at drug stores, grocery stores, etc. Its colors are usually enhanced: brighter and more intense than those on professional films (which tend to have more "normal" hues). Colors in amateur film can vary from batch to batch, from one roll to another. But this film is made so it will have a long shelf life in the shop, where it's stored at room temperature. Film begins fogging and deteriorating when its shelf life expires. Check the expiration date when you buy yours. And keep it out of the heat. If you've ever left a camera, or film, in your car in summer, you know what we're talking about. Cold temperatures slow film deterioration. It's a good idea to store film, especially if you have a lot of it, in the fridge or freezer. This is where you *must* store professional film.

You can find professional films in specialist photo shops and catalogs, bookstores at colleges with photography or journalism programs, and some regular photo shops. This film has a shorter shelf life and different makeup from amateur film. It's more sensitive to light levels, and made so colors in all rolls will match.

Carol-Lynn's favorite color film is a widely-available imitation black-and-white film. Its ASA is 400, faster and grainier than she usually likes. When processed, in the same chemicals as regular color film, prints done in studio situations look like sepia toned black and whites. Carol-Lynn prefers black and white to color because of its permanence and mystery. All color film (print and slide) fades. Properly fixed black-and-white prints retain their images, and seem to improve with age. Color images are formed with dyes. Black-and-white images are made from silver deposits.

LIGHT SOURCES

The secret to making "selling" photographs is not in fancy equipment, film speed or studio size. It is in the way you capture and manipulate the light source. The word *photography* means "writing with light." The kind of light you write with depends on your temperament, your surroundings, your aesthetic goals and your checking account.

AVAILABLE LIGHT

Photographers call regular daylight *available light*. When a piece is lit properly with available light like the kind that spills through windows onto an object (this is called "medium source light") shadows are gentle or nonexistent. The object photographed seems to glow with an almost other-worldly light, most appropriate for doll or teddy photos. Well-done available light photographs exude a gentle mixture of truth and mystery not produced by any combination of expensive artificial lights. They truly present your work in the best, "natural" light.

The trick is in learning to fool with mother nature and make her work with you *indoors*. You want to use *indirect* available light—the kind shining through your windows. Direct sunlight, especially the kind found outdoors around high noon, washes out highlights, creating dark, unflattering shadows. Don't use it for your studio shots.

Flattering available light outdoors occurs twice daily: at dawn (a gentle bath of blue), and just before sunset, starting around four o'clock. Photographers call this late, brief, warm glow "golden light." Landscape photographers say it's the day's best light. If you must photograph outside, choose a hazy day. Rush out right after the rain or in the mist or in the fog. Colors in photos taken in these circumstances are extraordinarily lovely; shadows are nil. No fog or rain? Find open shade: the area under a tree, or on a covered porch, *away from direct sunlight*.

ARTIFICIAL LIGHT

Artificial light is any light source other than the sun. There are several possible artificial light sources you might use to make your photographs. Each has advantages and disadvantages.

Camera Flash

You probably have a flash unit for your camera. Resist the temptation to use it when taking indoor studio shots of your dolls or bears. On-camera flash flattens and wipes out the area directly in its path. It causes harsh, ugly black shadows behind and sometimes on the subject. These effects can be minimized if you use a detachable flash unit—one not *on* the camera. This type unit lets you aim the light so it hits your subject in an indirect fashion. You want to bathe the whole area in light and to adjust any shadows, either to eliminate them or to make them fall in an enhancing manner.

Strobe Light

Professional strobe units consist of adjustable high-voltage power packs and connecting cables, two strobe lights (a main light and a secondary light), adjustable stands, and reflectors. A starter strobe system costs six hundred to one thousand dollars. Photos taken can be crisp, clean and mimic daylight.

Barb uses a *slave light*, a tiny, battery-operated unit, when she shoots indoors with artificial lighting. She aims the slave light behind her doll or bear and angles it to create the lighting effect she's after. When the main strobe flashes, it triggers the slave light to flash in synch and illuminates her shot from behind. This acts as a *hair light*, separating the subject from background.

Tungsten Light

Tungsten light is a more affordable option. Tungsten is the kind of light in ordinary indoor light bulbs. It has a yellow cast to it. If you take photographs indoors with daylight film and no flash unit, they will have an orangey golden tint. This is because the film "sees" the yellow in tungsten light for which our eyes compensate.

Tungsten light should be captured on tungsten film, which is not available everywhere. If you want to use tungsten light in your photo setup and can't get tungsten film, you can use a corrective filter over your lens to compensate for the "orange." Ask your camera store representative to suggest one for your camera.

For tungsten lighting, you will need at least two, preferably three 200-watt bulbs made specifically for photo lighting screwed into metal reflector pans. You must use photographic bulbs because the lighting temperature in them is specific and consistent. Unlike strobes, tungsten lights get hot in a hurry. This heat is sometimes so strong it can warm up the room: a problem in the summer, and sometimes dangerous.

Carol-Lynn has used three clamp-on screw-based light sockets for bulbs, with electric cords attached, into which she inserted photographic reflector pans and photo light bulbs. She would place two of them roughly at forty-five-degree angles at the front of the subject and one above and/or behind it, adjusting the light quality as the subject dictated. She would clamp the lights onto chair backs, lamp poles—anywhere she could find to allow them to point in the proper direction. Her total outlay, except for the special photo bulbs, was fifteen dollars.

FINDING A SPACE FOR YOUR STUDIO

We can hear you now: "Studio? What studio? There's no place here I can take studio shots."

Really?

Take a look at one of Carol-Lynn's studios. This spot is a corner of her enclosed front porch. It's unheated, squeezed between packing boxes. In winter, the temperature can reach thirty degrees below zero, and her only heating source is a small, probably dangerous, electric space heater perched on a wooden bench. This is where Carol-Lynn shot almost every cover of *Teddy Bear Review* for four years, and hundreds of editorial and advertising photographs, all of which were published, some of which won national photographic awards.

The walls are white, so they don't reflect color onto the model. To the right of and beyond her photo table (bought at a yard sale) are windows. She usually covers the window in back with cardboard or black fabric to prevent awkward lighting leaks.

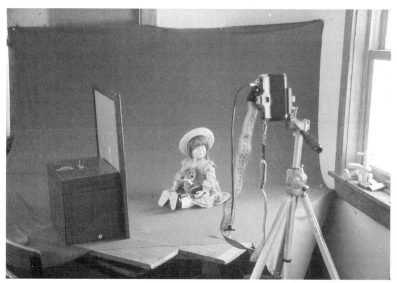

Carol-Lynn's makeshift front porch studio includes a seamless backdrop, a window for side lighting, a mirror reflector and a yard-sale table.

This winter she "moved up" to her kitchen. For six months, the kitchen table sat under an arch formed by the holder of a roll of seamless background paper. When she sat down to eat breakfast, she would play footsie with the electrical power pack to her lighting system and she had to be careful not to knock over the lights teetering on precarious metal supports. Most photos in this chapter were taken in the "kitchen studio" when she wasn't using the table for meals, sewing bears or painting fabric dye onto mohair.

If you want to try available light studio photography, find a spot near a window to set up your "studio." A tour of your house is sure to reveal some well-lit spot at least as glamorous as Carol-Lynn's. How about an area of your living room adjacent to a picture window, or a light-flooded dining nook? Do you have a spare bedroom, an enclosed front porch with windows, a well-lit attic or garage?

YOUR SURFACE

You will be setting up your work on a raised surface. This surface should be large enough to allow at least a foot and a half on either side of your creations and two feet behind and in front of them. Keep this requirement in mind when choosing studio space as well.

The higher up this surface is, the less your back will ache from bending over. The easiest surface to use is a table. You can buy portable picnic tables that fold up for storage. Portable fold-up cutting tables for sewing might work for you. Barb has used wooden TV trays, folding tables, and a length of plywood atop two saw horses. The table in Carol-Lynn's porch studio cost ten dollars at a yard sale. The surface in her kitchen "studio" cost considerably more, but it is used, occasionally, to serve dinner. Your surface does not have to be a permanent installation, like Carol-Lynn's, which will come down next Thanksgiving. Maybe.

Position your table so light falls on it from the front (good) or from one side (better). You need room to maneuver in front of, and on either side of, the table. You will be backing up, repositioning your camera, and taking close and distant shots. Don't box yourself in.

Your surface might still be too low for you to comfortably take photos, especially if your work is small. You can either bend over to reach it, or raise the work. To prevent backaches, look around the studio for possible risers. How about some cartons and a piece of plywood? A huge cardboard box? A footlocker? A coffee table? Whatever you choose has to have a flat top surface, and should be steady, sturdy and big enough to hold your photo setup. When you set up your tripod for your photo session, set up a chair next to it. Arrange your setups so you can see them from the chair by the tripod. After awhile, your back will ache if you stoop and bend to take your photos. Don't say we didn't warn you.

YOUR BACKDROP

In studio shots your job is to *emphasize the subject*, isolated from any distracting environment. No home decor, no "cute" settings. You are selling dolls or bears, not props. Anything extra in the photos takes attention

Carol-Lynn's teddy bear Carrie is photographed here on a dock in Maine. Notice how the cluttered background and shadow pull you away from your involvement with the bear, even though she is photographed at eye level.

from your work. To avoid this, surround your work with a consistent, easy-to-ignore flow of color.

This backdrop should start behind the photo table, high enough so it is out of camera range. Let it extend in a gentle flow atop your table surface and risers with ample margins on either side and let it drape down in front of the table, again, with ample margins. Here are some ways to get a plain, "invisible" background at little cost.

A matte (not shiny, not light reflective), non-textured, non-patterned, unwrinkled piece of fabric or paper going behind and continuing under the subject is best. Barb has used sheets, table cloths, lengths of fabrics and antique carriage robes. Velvet is luxurious and works well. As long as the fabric is pressed, it makes a decent background. Even the tiniest wrinkle will find its way into the wrong spots in your photos, and you won't see them until the photos have been developed.

Consider using a window shade. It comes with a dowel onto which it can be rolled and stored. You can mount it on a wall, behind your photo surface, making it easy to pull down over your table when you want to shoot. Non-glossy gift wrapping paper also works, as does poster board. Poster board absorbs light, so keep in mind the color of the board in your studio won't be what you see in finished shots.

Today, Carol-Lynn uses professional background paper for most studio

In contrast to the photo of Carrie on page 59, here she is photographed against a plain background, pulling you in with her eyes and allowing you to view her facial and costuming details.

shots. Seamless background is matte, sturdy, and feels like the construction paper you used in grammar school, only thicker. It is available in many colors. Seamless is non-reflective, so you won't get shiny spots in your shots. It is wrinkle-free and can be torn off and thrown away if soiled. It comes in a huge, wide roll reminiscent of a battering ram. The roll fits onto a stand adjustable for height and width. A stand and a couple half-width rolls of seamless cost around $150.

This stand suspends the paper above and behind the photo subject. Tack the fabric or paper to the wall at a height out of camera range, comfortably above your subject, about a yard from the back of the table. This creates some space between the backdrop and the table so the subject is not close enough to the backdrop to cast dark shadows. This also helps the background become just a surrounding hue.

CONTRAST
The color of your background should show off your subject to best advantage. Usually you want it to contrast. If you shoot a bride against a white

background, vital costuming details are bound to be lost. You'll probably want three shades of background: light, dark and medium-tone. Most practical are white, black and a medium gray. If you have money for one color only, try gray or a medium blue. Red backgrounds photograph a richer, deeper black than actual black in black-and-white shots.

Everything in black-and-white photos will be shades of gray. Combinations striking in color may not look right when printed in black and white. Editors may, without telling you, print your color shots in black and white in books or magazines. Color photo separations are expensive, and publications have limited budgets. Only the most striking shots, or those lucky enough to fall on designated "color pages," will be four-color, so consider this carefully when choosing a background color.

SETTING UP YOUR DOLLS AND BEARS

You've probably bought more than your share of products featuring photos of dolls or teddies in settings. Yes, these are "selling photographs." They sold you a tea tray, a puzzle, a calendar. But they didn't sell you any bears or dolls, did they? Photos like this compete in a different market from yours. By being warm, nostalgic and telling incomplete, romantic tales, they transport the customer into another place and time—one in which they can project themselves for a short time. Customers will buy everything from mugs to figurines as a ticket to getting there.

You say this is what you want to do. You don't. And you won't sell your bears with greeting card photos.

Your photo must grab attention, be impossible to ignore and, most important, engage emotions. You want to create an emotional urgency, an I-gotta-get-it mentality. There's a reason for the slogan, "Gotta Get a Gund."

To do this you must make the customers zero in on your doll or bear— *just* your doll or bear—as they flip through magazines or books or glance through junk mail. Anything extra in your photos will distract your customers' attention and lose you sales. Save the props for your next children's book or line of puzzles or greeting cards. Or for use as *size indicators.* Miniature artists sometimes photograph their work against pennies, thimbles, cookies or other small objects to show relative size.

Limit the number of dolls or bears in your photograph. The more in the shot, the more the viewer has to look at, the better the chance she won't look at what you want her to see. Photographing one doll or bear is best. Two is OK. Three is getting crowded. More than two subjects makes composition and focusing difficult. Just try to arrange three bears

This photo includes four bears of different sizes, all looking down at their cookies and coffee. Not only is the collector unable to focus on a single bear in this photograph due to the size differences and props, but she cannot see their lovable faces since all four are "ignoring" the camera. Such poses are not your best choice for advertisements and other promotional materials.

Because a close-up shot of a doll or bear makes it difficult for a collector to determine its size, artists who make miniature or small teddy bears or dolls often use props. This 2½" bear, Maria, is photographed alongside cutout cookies to demonstrate her relative size.

in the same "depth of field" so they're all in focus at the same time. The smaller the bears, the more difficult this is. A line of dolls can look like a theater queue. You want your creations to stand out, to be seen as individuals.

Position the doll or bear so it *looks into the camera.* You want your doll

This photo includes a total of nine bears. Notice how crowded the photo appears and how difficult it is to focus on a single bear's personality, even though they are all looking directly into the camera. You want your teddy bears to stand out.

These three bears still appear crowded.

It is best to photograph no more than two bears at once.

This bear, photographed alone, could win the heart of any collector because he is staring right into the camera.

to make intimate eye contact with the viewer. This will make your sale. Customers respond best to close-ups, to portrait shots. On the following pages, notice how much more involvement you have with Carol-Lynn's doll, Goldie, as the camera comes in close to her? You want the viewer to believe your work is real, that it might come alive and speak and respond.

The photographs through page 67, of Carol-Lynn's doll Goldie, show how, in many cases, moving in on the subject will increase the collector's feeling of engagement with the doll or bear.

LIGHTING THE PHOTOGRAPH

Available light isn't always available. The light doesn't always fall where you want, when you want it to. You must work with the light. Position your doll on the table so the light comes onto it from one side. Notice: One side of the head is light. One is dark, too dark. You're going to need to bounce light back into your set from your light source, the window. This is where your *reflector* comes in.

A mirror, a piece of cardboard covered with crumpled foil, a sheet of white foam core or cardboard can throw light back into your shot. Have at least two on hand. The reflector's size depends on how big your model is. One reflector should be a minimum of 11″ × 14″ in size. You'll need something to stand the reflector against, unless you have a studio assistant. You can see from the photograph of Carol-Lynn's porch studio she used a metal filing box.

A head-and-shoulders shot of Goldie.

Position your reflector on the side of the doll away from the window. Do you see what has happened? It has reflected some of the window light into the scene, brightening the far side of the picture.

The photo on page 68 is an example of "side lighting," the most dramatic type lighting you can use. It shows off texture, grain and profile. And, with your table near the window, side lighting is built in. The intensity of light can be varied by how close your put your teddy to the window. Practice with several rolls of film, taking notes of shutter speeds and f-stops, until you find a lighting design that works.

If you are working with artificial light, the position and angle of your lights will make all the difference in your photos. Start with the basic setup: one light on either side of the table at the front, turned at a forty-five-degree angle to the table. The lights, to start, can be above the subject, shining down. This should give you a balanced shot.

Move one light to the back, in stages, taking a shot of your doll or bear

Close-up of Goldie, focusing in on her face.

as you make each progressive move. Switch and do the same on the other side with the other light. Have the film developed and see what the moving lights do to the shadows on your model.

Lights from below give a late night horror show effect. Lights shining from on top are equally bizarre. Add a back light shining onto the back of the model from outside the photograph. Notice how it separates and isolates your subject. Move the back light up high, and you have a hair light which can add drama. Many photographers use this effect for portraits of people; fashion magazines are filled with them.

TAKING THE PHOTOGRAPH

You need a *tripod* to steady your camera. With a tripod holding your camera, you're free to concentrate on what's in the shot. You can hold the camera steady and at exactly the right height, time after time. And you

This doll exemplifies the dramatic use of "available light" side lighting. Notice that this is the same doll photographed in Carol-Lynn's makeshift studio shown on page 57.

can even put yourself into the shot if you use a *cable release* with a long remote cord to trip the shutter.

A cable release is a plunger-like apparatus on a cable cord. Cables come in lengths from six inches to several yards. The release plugs into the button you push to take photos and lets you trip the shutter without touching the camera. Because its touch is gentler than yours, it prevents camera wobble. This is important when you use slow film and available light.

A *light meter* can make the difference between a good shot and a great one. It can also save you reams of film. Your camera probably has a built-in meter. Use it for everyday shots. In the studio, you need to know what exposure to use to emphasize the most important parts of your photos, especially if you're shooting bears. Bear fur absorbs light and is a real pain to capture. You can live without a light meter and a tripod. Your photos may have more "life" if you use them.

In this photo, Goldie is facing center and the lighting is nearly equally balanced, making her appear less dramatic.

If you have a light meter, take a light meter reading of the subject: three readings, actually. One to the right, one to the left, and one in the center. Use the average of these readings as your camera setting.

Learn to see through the lens. Practice seeing your subject with all four corners of the camera's viewfinder. Really look at what is there, not with your imagination, but with the camera's eye. Use a lot of film; it's your cheapest tool.

Focus on the eyes. If they are in focus and other parts of your doll or bear are not, you may be forgiven. If the eyes are not in focus, the shot is lost. The eyes of your dolls and bears are the doorways to their souls. And if your viewers don't get in contact with your doll or bear's soul they'll never hear that "love me, I need you" message that will make your sale.

Know your camera's *depth-of-field* limitations. The depth of field refers to the part of the photo that's in sharp focus, and this is an important consideration. For example, it's possible to have the eyes in focus and the

These photos show how the use of light can change the way the viewer perceives a doll. In the photo at left, the light comes from the right-hand side and falls on only one side of her face, making her appear older. The photo on the right is more dramatic and makes her appear younger because the light illuminates her entire face.

end of the nose out of focus if the eyes are in the depth of field and the nose is not. This problem is compounded with each additional model in the shot, another good reason for shooting one bear at a time.

If your camera allows you to manually adjust the f-stops, *bracket* your shots. To bracket shots, take the same shot, after metering it with your light meter, at three or four different, adjacent f-stops. Start with the f-stop your light meter indicates. Then take a shot at one stop then two stops above that reading. Take a shot one stop and then two stops below that reading. This increases the chance you'll capture the perfect exposure for your setup and decreases the chances you'll have to retake the shots.

Make notes about each shot. This will be an invaluable guide when refreshing your memory about what works best under what conditions and with what type of film. Bracketing is especially useful when the object being photographed is very light or very dark, including black or white bears, black dolls and dolls wearing black or white outfits.

Whenever possible, compose and shoot your photos vertically. Vertical photographs have more power and are stronger visually. Horizontal compositions act as barriers, stopping the viewer's entry into the shot. If you shoot horizontals, you will usually end up with a lot of wasted space on either side of the bear. Of course, there are exceptions, like most of the photos illustrating this section.

Fill the viewfinder with your subject. This is probably the most important advice we can give you. Face your subject nose-to-nose. Unlike people, who grow queasy when you photograph them from six inches away, your bears or dolls won't peep if you get intimate.

Crop your photographs while they are still in the camera. Get rid of the white space around your subject. Design your shots, just like you do a painting or drawing. Give the viewer only what you want her to zero in on. If you leave it to a photofinisher to crop your work, you'll never get what you want. Your dolls do not need acres of breathing space around them. The more space around them, the smaller they're going to be in the photo. You want to give the viewer the most doll per square centimeter of photo.

Take full-lengths and closeups of each pose. Then photograph some details. Don't be afraid to cut off parts of the body or head. This should be done for a reason, though. Engage the viewer with each of your shots.

These full-length and close-up shots show how you can crop your photos while they are still in your camera to get the effect you want.

You can create an illusion the doll is alive if you position it in a ¾ pose, with the head slightly lowered and the camera's focus directly on the eyes. The emotional bond created by such a shot is powerful. Diagonals draw the viewer into your photograph, engaging him with your subject matter.

PROCESSING YOUR PHOTOS

Take your films to the best processing lab you can find. The corner drug store won't give you the quality you require. You will be amazed at the difference a professional lab makes. Shop around and compare quality and prices (this is where membership in the camera club comes in handy). Your choice of a film lab will depend on how much you want to spend and what is available in your area.

When you find a lab you like, stick with it. Get to know the people processing your film. If they know and like you and know what you want and why, they won't get overly upset when you tell them they have to redo the printing again because the color balance still isn't what you want or the print is too dark or needs spotting.

Relax. Take your time.

When you pick up you prints and they're just what you wanted, you can say, "I did it myself. It's darn good." And, despite your investment in equipment, you probably saved yourself a bundle—that bundle you never had to give the photographer downtown.

CHAPTER EIGHT

Media Publicity

*Y*ou've done research, attended shows, learned the players and the lay of the land. You've read magazines, books—everything about dolls or bears you can get your hands on. You've entered contests, donated bears to auctions, and you've joined organizations.

You've networked, networked, networked.

Still, you melt into the crowd of artists. Nobody besides the people you've met at shows—and sometimes not even them—knows your name. With budgets getting tighter, and more artists vying for fewer customers, if you don't stand out from the crowd, you might as well give up your doll making and get a "real" job.

How do you get people in other cities, other countries, to want your work, to seek you out, to recognize the name on your credit card? (Don't laugh: It happened to Carol-Lynn twice this year in shops in England.) What's an artist to do?

To cure those tired sales and flabby, ineffectual career plans, you need that recognition-enhancing, fortune-expanding, one-size-fits-many miracle product: media publicity!

PUBLICITY, NOT ADVERTISING

"But," you say, "I'm always going after publicity. I enter contests. I take out ads in all the magazines. Where's the big response for the money I spend? Seems to me, in these tight times, people play it safe and buy from name artists. I've done everything you told me to do to gain name recognition—advertised, lectured, researched, done workshops, entered contests, donated to auctions. What next?"

The next step is aggressively selling yourself and your product to the print media. We're not talking about advertising.

You buy advertising. Publicity is free.

Almost. You will pay for photos, the creation of your publicity materials and their mailing costs, and all expenses involved in your interviews or appearances. Compared to the cost of even one four-color magazine ad, you'll get great return for little cash outlay. Of course, there is a hidden cost: You'll be investing lots of energy, and time, to "spread the word." When you invest wisely, however, you will reap a great return. For your publicity campaign to be successful, you'll have to work with total commitment and with a strong belief in yourself and your product.

Remember, your customers are not just buying your dolls and bears. They are buying into you—into part of your story, your talent, your persona. Packaging is not a dirty word. In sales, it is everything. You must present yourself to the world in an attractive, professional, inviting package to be noticed. What are you going to put into this package?

THE PRESS KIT

A press kit is a folder filled with information engineered to give a writer, company, store or buyer a "take" on you and your work. Usually, all these people will know about you is what you include in this package. They won't have a lot of time to look at it, and are most likely swamped with dozens of things to read. You have to grab attention quickly, and present only the aspects of your story that are relevant to what you're selling.

A press kit should include the following elements:

- Photographs of your creations (for more information on taking such photographs, see chapter 7)
- A head-and-shoulder shot of you
- Tearsheets of articles by and about you that pertain to your involvement with dolls or bears
- A brief biography, focusing on your work and involvement with dolls or bears
- A resume (optional)
- A letter of purpose

Be sure all elements of the press kit relate to your work with dolls or bears. Don't confuse the reader with parts of your life that don't fit the story you want to tell. If you are a teddy bear artist as well as a champion ostrich raiser, for instance, you will want a separate press kit for each. Otherwise, a reporter may decide there are too many pieces to the puzzle and go on to something simpler. It's hard to fight the general perception that a person can do only one thing well: If she has a couple careers on the back burner, she's probably not serious about or not successful in either of them.

If you have never received coverage in any of the doll or teddy bear magazines, consider sending a press kit, along with a cover letter introducing yourself, to the editor. This is a good way to promote yourself initially, and any free press you can get from the magazines will be invaluable. Follow up this initial contact with press releases. See page 87 in this chapter for more information on writing press releases.

The best time to send a press kit to a reporter from a publication that is not doll- or bear-related, such as a local newspaper, is after the reporter has shown initial interest in you or your work. Generally, reporters do not have time to read a great deal of information about you, but if they read a press release and are interested in doing a story on the topic, you should offer to send your press kit to give more information about yourself and your work.

Press kits are not just for the press. They make for wonderful promotional packets to send to shops and doll and bear manufacturers interested in manufacturing your designs as well. See chapter 14 for more information on how to sell your creations wholesale, and chapter 15 on how to sell your designs to manufacturers.

GET YOURSELF "SHOT"

Besides the photographs of your dolls or bears discussed in chapter 7, you should also include a professional photograph of yourself. Decide, first, who you are and what kind of public image you want to present. Maybe you have several different audiences for yourself as "product." Steal an idea from professional models, who have on file a variety of publicity shots of themselves—formal, casual, business, full-length and head shots—and who send them out depending on the specific look an agency is seeking. For instance, you may want to send a different photograph to your local newspaper than you would to an upscale regional magazine or to a doll or bear magazine. On the other hand, if you have a limited amount of money, you may want to stick to one or two "classic" shots of yourself.

No, you can't use your high school graduation photo, or the snapshots from the last charity ball, no matter how lovely you look in your evening clothes. If you want to sell yourself to the media, you have to look professional. All they know is what they see and, yes, appearance does count. In show business, it's almost everything.

Where do you get these magical mug shots? If you live near a metropolitan area, check out local acting, talent and modeling agencies. Give each a call and say you're looking for a recommendation for someone who does great head shots. You don't have to mention you're not a potential client. If there are any beauty pageants in your area, organizers or participants can be great resources. They can tell you about a professional photographer in your area who takes publicity photos.

Going to a professional agency can get expensive. Such agencies may not be available in your area. If these are not options, ask around for names of good commercial portrait photographers, and make appointments to see if you like their black-and-white work. It's best to know the photographer's style, philosophy and policies before putting yourself in her hands. You're looking for the photographer who will present you in the best light, literally and figuratively. Lighting is everything in photography, especially black and white, and black and white, not color, is what you need. Keep interviewing candidates for your session with this in mind.

You've probably seen ads for national "glamour photography" chains. These create a good product, complete with high-pressure sales techniques to sell the instant-replay electronic proofs of your session minutes after you emerge from the studio. You don't have to spend a fortune, but remember that this is an investment in yourself and your business. If you can't afford the photographer you really want, consider bartering a doll or bear as all or part of the payment, if the photographer is willing.

When you interview photographers, ask about their policies. Be open about your needs, how much you can spend, and what you are going to do with the photographs. Most photographers, especially the glamour chains, ask you to sign an agreement when you arrange for your sitting. In it, they are trying to get the most mileage for their time and effort. And they are also trying to protect their copyright and control the use of their intellectual property. Most professional photographers nowadays have their photos printed on special professional papers that have a legend on the back reading, "Copyright protected. Do not reprint." You must obtain photos which can be reprinted without restriction. If the contract you are handed restricts you in your use of the photos, see if you can negotiate with the photographer. Get it in writing.

Some photographers, including all the photographic chains we've encountered, embed a nice little phrase in the contract saying your photos and any images they take of you can be used by them for any and all purposes without further compensation. If this clause bothers you, cross it out. Sometimes this clause ends up being advantageous to you, so weigh the benefits and liabilities.

Ask exactly what you're getting for your photo money. Will you have to do your hair and makeup, or will an assistant be provided for you? How long with the session be? How many poses and changes of clothing are involved? Will you get proofs, and when will they arrive? Can you get a special package rate? Is the photographer agreeable to giving you the negatives as well as the prints? Carol-Lynn knows of at least one Boston-based head-shot photographer who does a session involving two full rolls of thirty-six-exposure black-and-white film, and the client gets to keep all the negatives, for under two hundred dollars!

The good news is, you will need only one 8″ × 10″ print of each pose. Make sure the prints are not marked on the back with a reprint prohibition because you're going to have them reprinted in bulk—but elsewhere. Be sure this is not prohibited in your contract.

If you will have to do your own makeup, remember that makeup for photography is more dramatic than regular street makeup. Makeup for black-and-white shots is like stage makeup. If you don't use enough, you'll disappear, so don't be puritanical. This is your time to play dress-up.

THE HEAD-AND-SHOULDERS SHOT

What you want, first of all, is a good head-and-shoulders shot photographed against a light background. Wear appropriate clothing: a suit, blouse, shirt, or nice sweater—something not too casual but not too dressy, something in which you feel good about yourself. This will be your standard pose: nice, clean, clear, professional.

The head-and-shoulders shot below is a "one style fits most" type of

This is a classic head-and-shoulders shot.

photograph. You should have one like this in your press kit. Although this type of photo doesn't say anything about your line of business, it does say that you're serious about your image and that you are a professional. Carol-Lynn had this photo taken by a glamour photographer in Portland, Maine. He used a soft-focus filter on the shot. Carol-Lynn discovered this after the shot had been taken, and would not have permitted it had she known. A photographer uses a soft-focus filter to make the image less distinct, so wrinkles don't show and the subject looks younger. Some think the soft focus is dreamy or romantic.

Carol-Lynn was not interested in this. She wanted her head shot to reproduce sharply and clearly. While it does reproduce fairly well, it would have been much better without soft focus.

Notice: While Carol-Lynn faces the camera (with a slight tilt of her head to the left), her shoulders are at an angle to the right. This gives depth and dynamism to the pose, and is how you'll give life to your shots of dolls and bears as well. Use the exact techniques on them you'd use on a human model.

When a color shot is reproduced in black and white, it becomes "one generation removed" from the original and loses its quality. This is not the best way to go.

This shot began as a color print. Carol-Lynn sent it to a company specializing in printing head shots in bulk for professional actors and models. The firm shot a black-and-white negative and printed an 8″ × 10″ copy print. The firm used the black-and-white print to produce semi-glossy (luster) finish lithographic reproductions and imprinted Carol-Lynn's name in the white border below the image. Companies doing this sort of work offer a variety of type placements, styles and layouts, either free or at a low cost. They can add borders separating the image and the name border, like the hairline border here. These are nice touches and make the photos appear professional, but are not necessary.

Notice that the head shot is verticle. This is important. Verticle photos fit more easily in a column format. Editors will appreciate this.

In addition, follow all the tips given in chapter 7 for your own head shot: complimentary lighting, no props, and a plain background.

PHOTOS OF ARTIST AND CREATION

In addition to your head shot, you may want to have photos taken of yourself with one or more of your dolls and bears. The photos on the next two pages demonstrate a good and bad version of such a composition.

This shot demonstrates what you should avoid in a photo with your creations: a busy background, and bears or dolls that do not look at the camera.

Carol-Lynn no longer uses the above shot although she has 250 copies of it on file. Why? Let us count the ways!

- The focus is too soft.
- The photographer used the "no nose" technique currently popular with models and beauty pageant contestants. He used a soft focus filter with strong lighting to de-emphasize the nose, usually the least photogenic feature.
- The background is busy: The ferns distract the eye from the subjects.
- The bears aren't looking at the camera.

Carol-Lynn does use the shot on page 80. Why?

- The background is simple. The whole shot is a balanced mix of blacks and whites, focusing on the two sets of eyes making contact with the viewer. The white background in the upper corner mirrors the white in the lower left-hand corner.
- Carol-Lynn's doll, Nadezhda, looks into the camera.

You may want to have your name imprinted on your photo: Place it inside a white border, or directly onto the image, making it a borderless print with more image per square centimeter.

LABELING THE PHOTO

When sending a photograph of yourself or your work, you must identify it. Otherwise the person receiving it may not know what it is, especially

This shot is much better because it is photographed against a plain background, and the doll and bear are looking into the camera.

if it somehow gets separated from the rest of your material. Here is the standard format for labeling a photo: Type your name and all other pertinent data on a sheet of plain white paper. Using removable adhesive tape, attach it to the back of the photo. Fold the unused portion of the paper up and over the front of the photo. Make sure your caption always includes the name, address and phone number of a contact person.

Some people use clear address labels with their name, address and phone number on them, and place them in an inconspicuous corner (lower left) of the photo's back. This way, if the photo gets separated from the caption, the editor at least knows to whom it belongs. If you are sending several photos, you might number each caption and neatly write the caption number on the label.

Do not write on the back of the photograph. The writing may shine through and make it impossible to reproduce the print.

THE BIO SKETCH

Your bio sketch should be no more than one double-spaced page. It should include all the pertinent information about your work in the field, including the following:

- Your name and where you live
- When you began making dolls or bears
- A brief description of the type of work you do (mediums or type of fur used, size, style, etc.)
- A mention of any feature articles written about you

- Major awards and honors which you won or for which you were nominated
- Area of expertise
- Any special skills or programs you offer, including workshops, lectures, books, etc.
- Noteworthy recent activities within the field

Before you sit down to write, make a list of the aspects of your work that are unique. Your list might look like this:

- I only use high-quality mohair.
- My nose construction is different from most artists'.
- All my bears look contemplative and serious.
- All my bears wear hats I make myself.
- I make all their clothes.
- All my bears are little girls and boys.

Now, develop your paragraph, like this:

Jane Smith's original dolls are little girls and boys with contemplative expressions. They are made of fine porcelain and other high-quality materials. Jane has developed a clever, unusual method of body construction and articulation, giving her dolls lifelike posing possibilities. All Jane's dolls wear detailed dresses or suits which she designs and makes herself.

Next, list all your accomplishments, like this:

- Article in local paper about my workshops at local high school, January 1991
- Article in local paper about my lecture at senior citizen home, February 1992
- Feature article in *Dolls* about my fantasy line, August 1993
- Article in local paper about my demonstration for local Girl Scout troop, March 1994
- Nominated for *Dolls* Award of Excellence, 1995, 1996, 1997
- Won best of show at Colorado Doll Show, 1997
- Member of Colorado Doll Society since 1988

Here are some sample paragraphs based on this list:

Jane's dolls have been featured in *Dolls—The Collector's Magazine* and have been nominated for the *Dolls* Award of Excellence in 1995, 1996 and 1997. Her dolls have also won best of show at the Colorado

Doll Show in 1997.

Jane is a strong believer in educating the public about doll artistry and has presented demonstrations and lectures to high school students, Girl Scouts and senior citizens. She has been a member of the Colorado Doll Society since 1988. She lives in Boulder, Colorado, with her husband and three daughters.

Your bio should include only information relating to the doll or bear business, except perhaps your hometown and basic family information. ("She lives in Boulder, Colorado, with her husband and three daughters," for instance.) You may want to include a resumé rather than or in addition to a bio. But go lightly on "background." Editors want "foreground." "Why should I pay attention to this? Why would this person and what she does interest my readers and make them want to buy a copy of my magazine or newspaper?"

Carol-Lynn's standard bio is included on the following page as an example.

TEARSHEETS

Tearsheets are pages torn from articles by or about the person using them for publicity. Sometimes magazines will offer you a limited number of extra copies of such an article exactly like the originals. Usually you will have to photocopy the articles instead. For display at your booth at shows, include the actual article carefully removed from the magazine and included in a portfolio. As part of your press kit, however, photocopied articles will do.

Yes, this sounds like a catch-22. You can't have tearsheets for your press kit until you have sent out a press kit and received the coverage, can you? Yes and no. Yes, you can have a press kit without tearsheets. However, you should have something written about you—a short news piece for a magazine or local newspaper—to include with the press kit.

The best way to get your first tearsheet is to start locally. Approach a freelancer in your hometown. Become fascinating and indispensable, and you'll get coverage. Don't snort. This works. Your aim at the beginning is to have *anything* written about you so you can build an impressive paper trail. Carol-Lynn's daughter Jenny-Lynn did this in high school in an attempt to have articles for her portfolio, which she hoped would help her win scholarships and beauty pageants. It worked.

Carol-Lynn's father was wonderful at gaining publicity for the many organizations in which he was involved. When she started to make dolls

CAROL-LYNN RÖSSEL WAUGH
BIO SKETCH

Carol-Lynn Rössel Waugh began making dolls in grammar school and began her career as a doll and Teddy Bear designer in 1972. Trained as an art historian and photographer (her award-winning photographs of Teddies are considered among the best in the business) she carved a career by writing, with an insider's edge, about fellow designers and was the first to use the term "Teddy Bear Artist," in a *Doll Reader* article about doll artists who made Teddy Bears, in the early 1980s.

Carol-Lynn is associate editor for Fifth Avenue, New York-based *Teddy Bear Review* magazine, contributing articles and photographs. Her articles and photographs regularly appear in the major doll and Teddy Bear magazines.

Carol-Lynn made her first "artist bear" from porcelain in 1975, and is considered one of America's pioneer bear artists. Her first plush design, Yetta Nother Bear, made in 1985, was immediately accepted for commercial production and was distributed worldwide by England's House of Nisbit, in the first "artist collection" of Teddy Bears ever manufactured.

Gregory, a bear named for her brother, designed for Russ Berrie and Co., has proven Russ's best-selling bear in international markets. As a hand puppet, in his pilot uniform, Gregory flies exclusively on British Air. In 1996, Russ introduced Gregory's sister, *Greta* in three sizes. Carol-Lynn has designed many successful Teddy Bears for the Annette Funicello Teddy Bear Company, sold nationwide on QVC television.

Recently, Carol-Lynn went back to her "roots" and is again designing and making artist dolls. She hopes to connect with a commercial manufacturer to produce them in multiples for collectors.

Carol-Lynn still produces a limited number of handmade bears for collectors each year, but because of writing demands, prefers to concentrate on commercial production of her designs and to work with shops to create original editions specifically for them.

She lives in Winthrop, Maine.

CAROL-LYNN RÖSSEL WAUGH · 5 MORRILL STREET · WINTHROP, MAINE 04364-1220
PHONE: 207-377-6769 FAX: 207-377-4158

in 1972, he used the same tactics to help her gain recognition. He called a friend from "the lodge" who happened to be a photographer for the *Staten Island Advance*. This proves, again, that it helps to have contacts within the community. That afternoon, the photographer was at Carol-Lynn's house taking photographs of her dolls.

Once you have begun to collect newspaper clippings about your work, paste them on a clean sheet of white paper, along with a masthead from the newspaper including the name of the paper, the town and the date. You may need to shrink or enlarge the masthead and data to make everything fit on a page. If it is a long article, it is fine to continue the article on another page. Newspaper does not last forever, so it is a good idea to make a habit of cutting and pasting these clippings as they are printed, and immediately making several photocopies. Keep the original. Magazine articles can often be clipped from the magazine and photocopied as they are.

THE COVER LETTER

Never send a press kit without including a cover letter. This letter should be brief and professional. It should not repeat a great deal of information found in the kit, but simply state the reason you sent the material. The nice thing about cover letters is they can tailor the general press kit for a specific reason. See the examples of cover letters on the following pages.

Notice that all three of these cover letters are general in nature, providing enough information to pique the reporter's and shop owner's interest, but not enough to bore them. Also notice how each cover letter is personalized, including the editor's or shop owner's name and giving specifics about

---

DON'T FORGET TO SAY THANK YOU

After the *Staten Island Advance* printed the first article about Carol-Lynn's dolls, her father told her to write the photographer a thank-you note. Carol-Lynn will always remember what he said to her; it has ruled her behavior ever since. "Let these people [he meant the media] know you appreciate them for what they do for you. Always thank them. And mean it when you do. You will be one of the few."

Carol-Lynn has lost count of the number of articles the *Staten Island Advance* has written about her, even after she moved to Maine, when the paper continued to publish "local girl makes good" articles. Why did they continue to cover her? Perhaps because she took the time to say thank you!

COVER LETTER FOR SENDING TO A DOLL OR TEDDY BEAR MAGAZINE EDITOR

Dear [Name of Editor],

I have been making teddy bears for approximately two years. During this time, [name of magazine] has provided me with a great deal of information that has greatly enhanced my business opportunities. All my bears are my original designs and made of mohair and other quality materials. This press kit will give you more information about my work. Should you ever want to contact for me for more information, feel free to fax me at (555) 555-5555, send me an e-mail message at mydolls@aol.com or call me at (555) 555-5512.
Thank you for your time.
Sincerely,

[Your signature here]

[Your name here]

COVER LETTER FOR A PRESS KIT SENT TO A LOCAL NEWSPAPER

Dear [local news editor or features editor],

I am a doll artist who designs and makes original-art porcelain dolls. I have lived in Cincinnati, Ohio, for more than twenty years and have been making dolls for about ten years. As you will see from my press kit, my dolls have been featured in doll magazines and are sold in shops around the world, including All About Dolls in downtown Cincinnati. Several doll collectors in the Cincinnati area are loyal collectors of my work. I have given lectures about my work to young people in the Cincinnati public schools, and have demonstrated the doll-making process to the Women's City Club. During the summer, I travel extensively to shows in the tristate area and beyond.

If you are interested in learning more about me or my work, or would like to interview me for a feature article, please call me at (513) 555-5555. Thank you for your time! Sincerely,

[Your signature here]

[Your name here]

COVER LETTER FOR A PRESS KIT SENT TO A SHOP

Dear [shop owner],

I have been designing and making original mohair teddy bears for more than 10 years, but am just beginning to sell them in shops. Your shop was recommended to me by [name of another teddy bear artist who sells her work at this shop]. I have enclosed my press kit, which includes photographs of my most recent work. I am also open to creating a special edition for your shop, and would be available for signings and gallery showings.

If you are interested in selling my teddy bears in your shop, or would like more information, please call me at (555) 555-5555. Thank you for your time.

Sincerely,

[Your signature here]

[Your name here]

why you are sending the press kit to this specific magazine, newspaper or shop. The letter to the industry magazine mentions that the artist used this magazine to help her get started. It does not include information about how the artist makes or sells her creations because doll and teddy bear magazine editors already know this. The local newspaper letter focuses on local involvement. The letter to the teddy bear shop includes the name of the artist who recommended that shop. The cover letter allows you to personalize your press kit.

Typing a new letter each time you want to send a press kit is time consuming. You can save a template on a computer disk for each type of publication or shop to which you might want to send a press kit, then personalize it for each. Always keep records of who has received a press kit. You will want to follow up with a press release.

PRESS RELEASES

The best way to receive press coverage is to send a press release to magazines, newspapers and other publications each time you do something noteworthy in the industry. A press release is an article you write yourself in hopes the publication will either print it as is, rewrite it to fit space requirements, or—if you are lucky—call to arrange an interview about the event!

You are much more likely to receive coverage after sending a press release than after sending the more general press kit. This is because most publications prefer that even feature articles have some sort of current information. If a publication is interested in printing an article about you, they will undoubtedly call you after reading your press release. At this point, you should send the press kit before the interview so that they will have some background information about you.

Often what the media might consider noteworthy seems routine to you; at other times, it might be the other way around. Use your judgment. If you bombard the media with press releases, they will tire of hearing about you. But if you are selective, press releases will become your best asset. Here are some suggestions of events for which you may want to write and distribute press releases:

- You create a new line of dolls or bears.
- You donate a doll or bear to a charitable organization.
- You are participating in a show.
- You create a portrait doll.
- You receive or are nominated for an award.
- You are asked to participate in a gallery showing or artist signing.

- You complete a special edition for a shop.
- You are giving a lecture, workshop or presentation.

Use your judgment about when and where to send each release. If you are participating in a show in another city, send the release to the newspaper in that city. Do not send a release about a single show to a national trade magazine; the editor does not want to get a press release from every artist in the country each time they do a show. If you complete a special edition for a shop, make sure the newspaper in the town where the shop is located gets this information. If you are nominated for an award you will want to send releases to local media *and* national industry magazines (except, of course, the magazine sponsoring the award).

WRITING PRESS RELEASES

Writing press releases will become second nature once you begin. The important points to remember are the following:

- The press release should be as brief as possible, preferably no longer than one $8\frac{1}{2}'' \times 11''$ page, typed and double-spaced. If you use letterhead, make sure it looks professional.
- The words FOR IMMEDIATE RELEASE or, if it is time-sensitive information and cannot be used before a certain date, type like this: ADVANCE
  FOR RELEASE ON FRIDAY, FEBRUARY 29
- Under this heading, type the name and phone numbers of the contact person for the story.
- Skip a couple spaces, type your headline in bold caps, then skip a couple more spaces.
- The central purpose or most important news of the press release should be included in the first paragraph. This should then be followed with background information.
- The language should be simple and clear. Use strong, short sentences, vivid verbs and active voice. Avoid clichés.
- The release should be short and to the point.
- Proofread the press release for grammatical and spelling errors.
- To indicate the press release is finished, type one of the following journalistic codes for "the end." Center it at the bottom of the page, directly below the last paragraph:
  # # #
  -30-
  END

You may wish to accompany the press release with black-and-white photographs related to the event. For instance, if you are releasing a new edition at a show, include a photograph of that bear or doll.

If you are not sending a complete press kit, include a sentence or two of bio at the bottom of your press release. Expand, shorten, or personalize the message to fit your targeted market.

On the following page is a press release about Barb's work that led to coverage in more than thirty east coast newspapers. Several newspapers contacted Barb for further information and a photo. The press release appealed to a wide audience, including people who knew nothing about dolls but were interested in Vietnam affairs, nursing homes, fund raising, and the arts. You may recognize this press release from Barb's article in *The Doll Sourcebook*, but because it is such a wonderful example, we chose to reprint it here.

On page 92 is a press release about an event at which Carol-Lynn was honored. The press release led to coverage in five newspapers. A reporter from the *Bangor Daily News* asked for a press kit after reading the release, then arranged for an interview. This led to a two-page feature story that focused on Carol-Lynn's involvement with bears. In this case, the press release sparked a reporter's interest in Carol-Lynn's work and led to a great deal of free publicity.

Follow up press releases with a phone call. Offer to answer any additional questions the reporter might have or to schedule an interview. If the reporter seems interested, send a press kit to follow up your press release.

Publicity does not have to be costly. It requires little more than the confidence to let the media know what you are doing and a small initial investment of money and time. Go for it!

FOR IMMEDIATE RELEASE

Local Artist Honors Vietnam Veterans
Local sculptor and internationally known doll artist Barb Giguere of Scarborough, Maine, has released two new one-of-a-kind dolls which will be exhibited at the Doll & Teddy Bear Expo '95 in Washington, DC. The dolls, which reflect the trauma of the Vietnam War, will be donated to raise money for a stress-management program for the staff of the Maine Veterans Home in Scarborough.

One of the dolls is modeled after a disabled veteran. He is a double amputee sitting in a wheelchair, obviously suffering from post-traumatic stress disorder. The other doll portrays a U.S. Army nurse returning to the States with the young veteran.

Barb visited Washington, DC, following the unveiling of the Vietnam Veterans Memorial. The memory of a young veteran she saw there has remained with her for more than twelve years. She had to memorialize this soldier as a doll. Her mother, a World War II Army nurse serving in Europe, was the inspiration for the other doll.

Many local people helped make these sculptures a reality. Whity Bearisto of Mark It With A "B" in Stratham, NH, made the wheelchair. Jerry Thomas supplied the desk-sized POW-MIA flag, which is displayed on the back of the wheelchair, and the U.S. flag, folded as is proper for a funeral, which the veteran is holding in his lap. The dog tags worn by both dolls were engraved by Classic Impressions of Portland, Maine.

These dolls will be posed in front of a large photo of the Washington, DC, Statue of Three Servicemen, which represents three U.S. soldiers in Vietnam. The photograph was donated by another Vietnam veteran. The nurse's pin and lieutenant bars were worn during World War II by the artist's mother, who was a resident of the Maine Veterans Home in Scarborough until her death last month.

END

ADVANCE
FOR RELEASE ON MAY 7, 1996

Children's Home Honors Local Writer and Designer
Carol-Lynn Rössel Waugh of Winthrop, Maine, renowned Maine
writer, doll and teddy bear designer, and artist, will be the honored
guest at a Blaine House tea at the Governor's Mansion on Wednes-
day from 2-3:30 P.M.

The annual event brings the constituency of the Maine Children's Home for Little Wanderers together with unique people
who exemplify the best in Maine. The public is invited. Reservations
are suggested by calling 555-5555.

The purpose of the tea is to draw attention to the Maine Children's Home for Little Wanderers, a nonprofit agency with offices
in Augusta and Waterville. The agency works to benefit children
and families in need throughout Maine, providing counseling,
foster-care homes, and programs for single parents and young fa-
thers, as well as a summer camp and Christmas program.

The agency chose Waugh as honored guest in part because of
her work with Russian children. Waugh first visited the former
Soviet Union in 1990 with the Maine Bridges for Peace group.
On her second trip, in 1991, she met many children in orphanages
there and, upon her return to Maine, arranged for shipments of
teddy bears for some of the orphans.

A freelance writer, photographer and designer, Waugh has written
six books and coedited sixteen others. She has had hundreds of articles
and photos published in national magazines and has won numerous
awards for her writing and photography from the National Federation
of Press Women. She was named Maine's Communicator of Achieve-
ment by the Maine Media Women in 1992.

A commercial toy designer since 1986, Waugh has had her work
manufactured by the House of Nisbet in Great Britain, Effanbee
Doll Company, Bearly There, Russ Berrie and Co., and Knicker-
bocker Creations. Her bear designs for the Annette Funicello Teddy
Bear Co. are sold on QVC Television and at Disney theme parks.
Her Russ Berrie bears are sold worldwide. She also produces handmade dolls and bears for collectors each year.

-30-

CHAPTER NINE

Facing Broadcast Media

ost of your contacts with the media will be with print media, but occasionally you may have to face radio or TV reporters. Have you ever been at a show, minding your own business, and suddenly had a cameraman point his video camera at you and ask about the heads on your dolls, and seen yourself three hours later as part of a feature on the local newscast? Those fifteen seconds of fame don't happen very often, but you should be ready when they do.

In case you are asked to say something on camera at a show or public event, you will always want to look your best. The best way to prepare for this is to videotape yourself responding to questions. Have a friend act out the part of the reporter. Go over the videotapes. Are you slouching, or pushing your hair out of your face from nervous habit? Cameras pick up on everything. Keep practicing. Learn to answer questions on the spur of the moment. The more you practice, the more comfortable you will become.

PITCHING TO A BROADCAST STATION

If you are interested in being interviewed by a broadcast reporter, watch or listen to the TV and radio stations in your area. Get to know the types of newscasts these stations have. You will be most likely to land a spot on a public-access TV or radio station. They hold interview shows focusing on people in the community. Send your press kit or a press release to the station just as you would to a newspaper or magazine. Barb's interview resulted from community requests following a presentation at the library. It's best to start small, then move to your local network-affiliate station's news show or a radio show with a wider audience.

Include a pitch letter with the press kit. This pitch letter should briefly and succinctly state who you are and why it would be to the station's advantage to have you on a specific program. Include when you will be available, as well as your name, address, and phone and fax numbers.

PREPARING FOR A BROADCAST INTERVIEW

If you are offered an interview, you will have to do some homework. Think about what you would like the reporter to ask you. Prepare a list of suggested questions to give to the reporter. These questions should require some thought. They should not be yes-and-no questions. Organize these questions according to topic, and neatly type them. The reporter may not ask all the questions on the list, or may throw in some questions for which you are not prepared, but she will be thrilled to have something to start with.

Along with the list of questions, you will want to prepare a card on which your name is spelled phonetically, especially if your name is hard to pronounce. You may want to include a reminder to the host about why you are here. Occasionally you will get an unprepared host who has no idea. For instance:

Carol-Lynn Rössel Waugh (pronounced Russel Waw—rhymes with coleslaw).

Local doll and teddy bear artist who will be conducting a workshop at the local teddy bear show on Friday.

Second, make sure you are clear on what is required of you and what to expect. Find out how long you will be on the air, what you should wear, and where you will be filmed or recorded. Will you have to come into the studio, or will it be an on-location interview? How many people will be watching on the set? Ask if you will be permitted to give a demonstration and to bring visuals.

Be sure to watch the show on which you will appear several times before your interview so you'll have an idea of the show's format and the personality of the host. Is she very serious, or do the interviews tend to be light and playful? Will you be the only guest, or will you be on a panel?

Be prepared to look your best on camera. Dress casually but nicely, unless the show has other requirements. If you wear a skirt, make sure it covers your knees when you sit. Wear medium-range colors that best show off your skin tones. Avoid vivid colors, (they bleed on camera) or pale colors (they make you look heavier). Whatever you do, do not wear white. TV cameras cannot handle it.

SAMPLE PITCH LETTER

Dear Mr. Johnson,

I am a local doll artist who has received a great deal of national exposure within the past two years. I have won two top industry awards and have been asked to speak about my work at more than ten shows across the country. Next month I will be conducting a three-day doll-making workshop at City Technical College. Over fifty people are signed up for the workshop.

If you are interested in interviewing me about my work in the community, please call me at (555) 555-5555 or write to me at the address above. I will be available for an interview any weekday evening this month. Thank you for your time.

Sincerely,

Jane Smith

EXAMPLE QUESTIONS FOR A
BROADCAST INTERVIEW

BREAKING INTO THE BUSINESS:
- When did you make your first teddy bear?
- Did you expect to become a full-time teddy bear artist?
- Do you have any special training?
- What other jobs have you held?

THE CREATIVE PROCESS:
- How long does it take to make a teddy bear?
- What materials are needed?
- What skills are needed?
- How do you come up with new designs?
- What is the difference between a mass-produced teddy bear and an artist-made teddy bear?

WORKSHOPS:
- How many workshops do you do per year, and where are they held?
- How long do they last?
- What is covered in the workshops?
- How many people usually attend?
- How much do they cost?

CHALLENGES:
- What do you find most difficult in creating teddy bears?
- What are some misconceptions others have about your work?
- What is the most difficult part of selling your creations?

OTHER:
- Have you ever considered selling your designs to a manufacturer? Why or why not?
- What advice would you like to give to others attempting to break into the teddy bear business?

> ## QUESTIONS TO ASK THE SHOW CONTACT ABOUT A BROADCAST INTERVIEW
> 1. How long will I be on the air?
> 2. How many people will be on the set in this segment?
> 3. Will I be asked to give a demonstration?
> 4. Will I be part of a panel?
> 5. Are there dress requirements I should know about?
> 6. Is this in studio or on location?
> 7. Will this be a serious interview, or will it have a lighter format?
> 8. May I bring and use visual materials?
> 9. Can I have a copy of the broadcast tape? Is there a cost? Shall I bring my own tape?

You will need to wear more make-up than usual. Use matte earth tones. Try brown lipstick within clearly drawn lipliner. Grey and brown eye shadow broadcasts best. Do not use frosted eye shadow or lipstick, red lipstick, or blue eye shadow. These scream and bleed on camera.

PRACTICING THE INTERVIEW

Practice. Don't even think about going on cold. Answer each question you are offering until you can do so effortlessly. When you are sure what you want to say, have a friend act out the part of host. Videotape or audiotape the interview. Study the tape. What needs more practice? Did the tape help you notice annoying nervous habits you have, such as constantly saying "uh" or moving your foot back and forth? Cameras catch the smallest flaws. Keep practicing until you like the way you look and sound.

Expect your host to throw in a few questions you were not expecting. Have your friend act out different kinds of hosts: hosts who try to get you off the subject, who are confrontational, who try to make you feel uncomfortable. You never know if you will have to face these situations. Practice steering the conversation back on track by saying something like, "I'm really not prepared to talk about that, Jim, but I think our listeners might be interested in a related topic. I was hoping to talk not about why my dolls are more expensive than Sally Smith's, but about the kind of work that goes into making an original porcelain doll. By explaining this, I think everyone will understand why I price my dolls the way I do." It's impossible to be prepared for everything, but the more you practice handling unexpected questions and situations, the better skilled you will be!

Videotape yourself wearing the clothing and makeup you plan to wear on the show. When you review the tape, you may find your favorite dress does not look right, or the eye shadow you always wear does not flatter you on camera. This is the time to make adjustments. The more you've practiced, the better off you are!

CHAPTER TEN

Advertising

e can hear you now. "I can't afford to advertise!" The fact is, you cannot afford not to advertise if you want to be successful. Advertising is as much about achieving name recognition as it is about selling the product that appears in the advertisement.

IMAGE IN ADVERTISING

Remember that any advertising you do is a projection of your image as well as a presentation of your doll or teddy bear. Are you flamboyant? Is your work dramatic? Then you certainly don't want your advertising to project a flat, mundane image, do you?

Are you and your dolls or teddy bears associated with a vintage look? That same feeling should carry through in each advertisement. Do you specialize in a Christmas theme? You will want that to be quickly recognized in your ads.

Christie Cummins is a strong believer in artists doing their own advertising. Christie's ads have produced wonderful results for her. They are almost always head shots or the head and upper torso with the words *Christie Cummins Dolls* and her phone number superimposed over the photograph. She carried through with this style at Toy Fair by displaying a poster-sized color photo of one of her dolls at her booth space. Instant recognition! From a distance, there was no question who was in that booth.

Go back to your research. Take note of advertising that has caught your eye. What drew you to the ads? Look for these artists at shows. How do their ads reflect what you see in person? You can do this for other artist-created products, too. Is there a local jewelry designer, sculptor or potter who advertises in your regional newspaper? Take time to see her creations first hand.

Make sure your advertising style is as original as possible. Avoid copying aspects of someone else's ad. You don't want to confuse the reader and promote someone else!

BLACK-AND-WHITE VS. COLOR PHOTOGRAPHS

A word of advice: If you are using color photos of your work in your ads, you will need quality color photographs to start with. If you choose black-and-white ads, submit black-and-white photographs. Barb and Carol-Lynn recently spent an evening critiquing magazine ads. Every time Barb found a particularly poor representation of a known artist's work, Carol-Lynn studied the photo and said, "It probably would have looked nice in color." Color photos of the blond doll or light-colored teddy bear probably did look nice with the soft blue background. But they washed out dismally when printed in black-and-white ads.

Paid advertising costs are based on the size of the ad space. There is one cost for black-and-white and a higher cost for color. If your doll or bear will not look right in black and white, it is better to pay extra costs and have a nice looking advertisement than to have your creation appear washed out or unclear. You are paying these costs and you are responsible for the photos you submit for these ads, so make sure you make the right decisions.

MAGAZINE ADVERTISING

Magazine advertising is perhaps the best way to reach the largest number of collectors at one time. When you advertise in the national doll and teddy bear magazines, your work reaches a huge geographical area, allowing collectors to contact you with an order for a specific doll or teddy bear. Magazine advertising also works to enhance your name recognition. Even if a collector is not interested in a particular doll, she will recognize the quality or style of your dolls, and remember your name. This may lead to future sales.

Magazine advertising reps will help you create your ads if you are not sure what you want or how to present them. If you know exactly what you want, and can submit camera-ready copy, then be sure to ask for the appropriate discount, which is usually 15 percent. If you don't ask, you may not get it.

If you are going to advertise in magazines, do it frequently. Like frequent flyers, frequent advertisers pay less. In addition, the more often a subscriber sees your ad, the more likely she is to remember your name and your teddy bear or doll. Advertising only once a year in a magazine will probably not be worth your money. In fact, the first ad you run probably will not greatly enhance your sales. But if that ad appears again and again, collectors will notice, remember and buy!

Judging by our own data and the data of the Maine Society of Doll and Bear Artists, there is far greater response to advertisements and articles in teddy bear magazines than to advertisements and articles in doll magazines. We won't attempt to explain this—we are only noting it as a fact to be considered. (No, we do not think that dolls should be advertised in teddy bear magazines. This would be a waste of money!)

ADVERTISING COSTS

Know your advertising costs and realize that they must be recouped through the sale of your dolls and teddy bears. Suppose you can buy advertising space in six magazines a year at a cost of $2,400, so you are spending $400 per ad. If you advertised a different one-of-a-kind in each of these six advertisements and sold only those six dolls or bears that year, you lost a great deal of money. The entire cost of one entire ad, $400, would have to be built into the cost base of each doll or bear. On the other hand, if you sell fifty dolls or teddy bears that year, you have a built-in magazine advertising cost of $48 for each one!

You're probably thinking, "But I advertised an edition of five dolls or teddy bears in each of six ads. Doesn't that mean the $2,400 advertising costs were for thirty dolls or teddy bears and not fifty?" No. Your advertising costs in one year are spread among the dolls or bears you *sell* in that year. You're advertising yourself, your product line and your company in each ad, not just the item pictured. What happens if the doll or teddy bear in the ad has sold out when the collector contacts you? Do you say, "Sorry, I can't sell to you"? Of course not! You offer to send photos of other work! You can see that an ad works for all your creations, not just one.

GROUP AND CO-OP ADVERTISING

One way to reduce advertising costs is through group ads. Several artists share the expenses for one ad. Two quarter-page ads cost more than one half-page ad. You can grab more reader attention through the larger ad while reducing your costs. Another possibility is co-op advertising with shops. Manufacturers do this frequently. Whenever the shops advertise a doll or teddy bear and include the manufacturer's logo or trademark, the manufacturer pays a portion of the advertising cost. You can approach any shop that buys your work about co-op advertising. You may be pleasantly surprised.

Don't do as one artist did several years ago. The artist offered the doll to the shop for no cost if the shop would include a photo of the doll in one ad. This didn't make any sense because the doll wholesaled for well over five hundred dollars, and the shop consistently presented six tiny black-and-white head shots of dolls in each ad with a total ad cost under five hundred dollars. The artist could have placed a larger ad, including address and phone number, for the same dollar amount, attracting far more attention from collectors and other shop owners.

SHOW PROGRAMS

While show programs do not reach as many people, advertising in them is less expensive and may be worth the money. Because show programs are often mailed to collectors and retailers in advance, those attending the show will be more likely to visit your booth if they see the advertisement. In addition, most shop owners and collectors will save and refer to the ad after the show is over.

Before submitting photographs for a show program advertisement, ask if the program will be printed or photocopied. Volume photocopying does not satisfactorily reproduce photographs. It would be better to include only your business card or company name, logo and text in an ad to appear in a photocopied show program. For printed programs, find out if the program will be printed in black and white or color so you can be sure the photographs you choose will be appropriate.

COMPUTER ADVERTISING

In today's high-tech world of scanners and computers, there are many different promotional opportunities for dolls and teddy bears. Promoters are creating and distributing their own catalogs of artist originals. At least one company is producing and selling a CD-ROM with photos and information about artists' dolls at a nominal cost per doll.

Many artists are taking advantage of the World Wide Web on the Internet. Web page design services are widely available, and several teddy bear artists have created their own Websites. They have found this a profitable and affordable way to reach collectors. An advantage to having a Web page is that you know how many people have looked at your page because the system records the number of "hits" each page gets. Prices for Websites vary, so investigate options in your area before committing to a long-term contract.

Advertising is a wonderful way to reach collectors and build name recognition. Advertising costs can easily get out of control, however, so set a limit on your advertising expenses over a given time period.

PART THREE

Selling Methods

CHAPTER ELEVEN

Selling by Direct Mail

*S*elling your dolls and teddy bears by direct mail allows you to reach a customer base you otherwise might not reach. It is both a selling method, and a publicity method. Even if you do not receive orders from everyone who receives a mailing, continued mailings will keep your work in the minds of collectors and past customers, making it easy for them to reach you.

Selling by direct mail should be used in addition to selling at shows. This way, you can reach those not attending the shows in which you participate, and inform those signing your guest book at shows about new dolls or bears or upcoming show participation.

DEVELOPING A MAILING LIST

If you are selling your teddy bears and dolls wholesale, develop your own mailing lists of shops by studying ads in the magazines and by collecting business cards. (You have been collecting business cards, haven't you?) Remember, your mailings to shops must include your wholesale prices, not your retail prices!

Developing a collector mailing list takes more work. This is where the value of a guest book pays off. The collectors who sign your guest book at shows want to be on your mailing list. They are requesting information about your dolls or teddy bears. Include those who have bought from you. Some collectors select artists whose work they really like and collect only their dolls or teddy bears.

If you want to reach a larger number of collectors, you may want to consider sharing mailing lists with other artists or buying mailing lists from show promoters or the doll and teddy bear magazines. Many shops extend their customer base by purchasing mailing lists.

Most computer databases allow you to print labels or envelopes. Some have mail merge features, allowing you to personalize standard letters. They work wonderfully for record keeping as well. Include the date the shop or collector was added to the list and a system for keeping track of how often they order from you. This way, you can remove people from your list who have been receiving mailings for over two years without ordering a doll or teddy bear from you.

TYPES OF SALES LITERATURE

There are several different types of sales literature to use. Your choice will depend on how much you depend on direct-mail sales, how much you want to spend, and how often your product selection changes.

PROFESSIONALLY PRINTED LITERATURE

Professionally printed literature can range from one-page flyers to color catalogs. Professionally produced color catalogs, complete with photos of your dolls or bears and an order form, while beautiful, are expensive. Professionally produced black-and-white catalogs cost less, but are still costly. Few doll and teddy bear artists go this route.

If you are counting on direct-mail sales for the largest portion of your business, catalogs may be worth the expense. However, putting together a catalog with text, photos and an order form, and finding a printer to produce the number of catalogs you need at the cost you can afford is time consuming and expensive. To make a catalog cost-effective, you must have a product line, complete with samples of every limited edition you plan to make, ready and photographed before you begin to put the catalog together. This takes careful planning. If you make mostly one-of-a-kinds or special orders, a catalog is useless because it will soon be outdated.

A professionally produced flyer (color or black-and-white) is an option. Flyers are 11″ × 17″ or 8½″ × 11″ sheets of high-quality paper professionally printed with photos of your products and text on one side, and an order form on the other side. Some flyers include all product information and photos on side one, and an order form, a blank space for the address label and postage, and your name and address on side two. This way, the order form on the flyer can be easily folded and returned to you. If you use this type of flyer, you will need to accept credit cards. Otherwise, the customer would have to use an envelope in order to include the check, and this would make printing your address futile.

Flyers are cheaper to produce than full catalogs. They're better for artists who do not make enough dolls or bears to fill a catalog or who want to produce sales literature as they create. Rather than sending one catalog to everyone on the mailing list once a year, artists who use flyers can send them three or four times a year as their selection changes. Less expensive than professionally produced catalogs, these professionally produced mailers are still costly.

SELF-PRODUCED SALES LITERATURE

Self-produced literature is the most cost-effective method and is most commonly chosen by doll and teddy bear artists. Some artists choose to produce their own literature using color copiers. Others prefer to send photos along with a personalized form letter.

Compare the cost of color prints to color copies in your area. Anne Cranshaw and Debbie Lane use color copies for their mailings, and while some argue that the quality is not as good as color prints, the mailings are less expensive and work well for their purposes. If you choose to make your flyers, arrange six color photos, along with the appropriate information, on an 11″ × 14″ sheet of paper. Include your name, address, phone and fax numbers, and, if space allows, an order form. The copy center can reduce this to an 8½″ × 11″ flyer. Make the layout of your literature uncluttered, with a balance between photos and print. Keep it simple. Do not tell the collectors or shop owners more than they need to know.

LETTER AND PHOTOGRAPH MAILINGS

If you send photographs, attach information about the doll or teddy bear along with your name, address, phone and fax numbers to each one. Include a letter introducing yourself and your work to the collector or shop owner. Actual photographs are better quality than color copies, but more expensive.

In your letters include information about the dolls or bears you are selling and general information about yourself. Have separate letters for retailers and collectors. If you have a mail merge function on your word processor, you can merge names from your database with a form letter, personalizing each letter. A sample follows on the next page.

Notice how this letter briefly describes each doll, gives a small amount of background on the artist, and includes an invitation to contact her. A letter like this, along with good-quality photos of the dolls you are interested in selling, will be welcomed by shop owners.

If you are sending photos to collectors, send a letter similar to the one just mentioned, along with an order form to reserve a doll in one of the editions, or an invitation to call with an order. Be sure to include the retail rather than the wholesale price.

SAMPLE LETTER TO SHOP OWNER

Dear [name of shop owner here],

I am writing to tell you about two new limited-edition dolls not yet released to the public. The first, Maria, is a beautiful Hispanic woman designed after my daughter. She has long black hair and a flowing red dress designed and made especially for her. The second, Jessica, is an African-American toddler with curly hair wearing a short white dress, pink bib, and white shoes. Both are 10″ porcelain dolls and come in limited editions of twenty. They sell for a wholesale price of $400 each.

My high-quality dolls have been sold in shops across the country for five years. Their wistful expressions and carefully designed clothing have won the hearts of collectors everywhere. Each comes with a certificate and silver charm. I have enclosed photos of these dolls.

If you are interested in carrying one of these dolls in your store, please contact me at the address or phone number above. Thank you for your consideration.

Sincerely,

[Artist's name here]

ORDER FORMS

It's *not* a good idea to include order forms with mailings to retailers unless they are for dolls or bears already produced. In mailings to retailers, include your name, address, phone, fax and e-mail information so they can contact you about purchasing creations you've completed or ordering your creations. Before selling your creations to a retailer, discuss an order thoroughly and draw up a contract. For some more tips on this, read chapter 14.

Mailings to collectors can include either information so that a collector can contact you by phone or fax to express interest in ordering one of your dolls or bears, or an order form. Order forms make this simpler; take care to design them well. Include the name and price of each doll. Leave a space to calculate the sales tax. Anyone purchasing a doll or bear by mail must pay sales tax if she lives in the same state as the seller or in a state in which the seller holds a sales tax permit/license or resale number. Make sure this is explicitly stated on the order form. Include a space to calculate the total.

Be sure there is a space on the order form for the customer to circle or check their method of payment. Do not accept cash through the mail. If you accept credit cards, include names of the cards you accept and space for the customer to fill in the card number, expiration date and signature. Include a statement saying you will charge the amount to the credit card prior to shipping. This gives you the chance to make sure the card is legitimate. If you accept checks, leave a space on the order form for the customer to check or circle "check enclosed." Include a statement saying you will ship after the check has cleared. For more information on accepting checks and credit cards, see the discussion of methods of payment in chapter 13.

BROCHURES AND FLYERS

Consider brochures and flyers meant to update collectors on your work rather than sell new creations. These can easily be reproduced at a regular copy center, distributed at shows and through the mail. The copy center staff will copy and fold brochures for you. These brochures are excellent for show lists and similar information. Some artists produce newsletters to keep past customers updated about new work, shows and other events in which they will be participating, and other information.

Most artists in other fields use advertising brochures or flyers which they distribute at shows and use as mailers to collectors, shop owners and show promoters. Whenever you will be distributing your own advertising materials, remember: Presentation is everything. A few extra dollars for quality paper makes a huge impact on the person receiving your promotional materials. You want them to remember you. For more information on promotional materials and selling your products via direct mail, see chapter 11.

Affordable computer programs that allow you to lay out newsletters and other sales literature on screen are readily available. They come with several fonts and size ranges for text and graphics. If you do not own such a program or a computer, you can rent time on a computer at most copy centers. Usually these centers are equipped with such programs, and employees can help answer your questions. You can purchase blank tri-fold brochure paper stock at many office supply stores. There's no excuse for not taking advantage of these sales tools.

If you have a computer, take the time to enter your mailing list into a database which allows you to sort the list by state. Depending on the size of the mailing list and how much you want to spend, you may have to modify each mailing to reach potential customers in a certain geographical area. To send notice of your participation in a show, you could mail only to those collectors most likely to attend that show—those living in the same state and surrounding states.

DIRECT-MAIL COSTS

Direct-mail costs add up quickly. Shopping around is important. You will want to find the best cost for every aspect of your mailing, from labels to color copies. Office supply stores sell envelopes and labels in bulk. If you want envelopes and stationery printed with your logo, have them printed in bulk—it costs much less.

If you have a mailing list of two hundred, you will need two hundred sets of information, address labels, envelopes and postage. Six-by-nine-inch manila envelopes are available in boxes of one hundred and five hundred. They can hold a full page folded in half and photographs of this size for a two-ounce postage charge.

You should weigh the cost of mass mailings with the anticipated responses. Five percent is the average mail order response. How many dolls or bears do you have to sell to recoup your mail order investment?

If you plan your mass mailing (500 pieces or more at one time), and if you intend to do more than one in a calendar year, contact your local postal service customer service business representative. The postal service offers reduced rates for bar coding volume mailings. We recommend First Class mail, not Bulk Rate, because the delivery priority for Bulk Rate is less than desirable. The postal service does charge for this service. Unless you can project a true savings, don't spend the money and time.

Another mail order option is offered by mailing services. These companies package numerous offers into one mailing and target geographically oriented customers.

SHARING COSTS WITH OTHER ARTISTS

Joining forces with other artists will cut costs. Make sure your business is organized. One person must be responsible for collecting materials and money for envelopes, address labels and postage. Someone must take on the responsibility of designing the catalog or flyer and overseeing production. Preparing the envelopes and mailing the literature can be a much greater undertaking than you imagined! The person doing the coordinating must set deadlines the others must meet to get the mailing out in a timely manner.

FILLING ORDERS

Once you have completed a mailing, be prepared for orders! Take time to keep records of these orders, and to fill them. If you included order forms, call to let the collector know you received the order, and note the date the order was received in your database or other records. Whether a collector orders by phone or mail, note approximately how long it will take before she receives the bear or doll. If you are doing a limited edition and get more orders than you have dolls or bears, contact the collectors and let them know the edition is sold out. Offer to send photos of similar creations.

Another great way to reach collectors is by including a sneak-preview photo of your latest work in thank-you notes sent to each collector when she has bought a doll or bear from you. You are sending thank-you notes, aren't you? Remember, it's the happy customer who comes back again and again!

SHIPPING AND PACKAGING

There are many ways to ship your dolls or bears. Dolls are fragile and should be shipped expediently—never longer than second day air if possible. UPS offers second day air and can track your package. Federal Express offers second day economy and many artists find this the most satisfactory shipping method. Other doll artists prefer Express Mail through the U.S. Postal Service. One advantage of Express Mail is that delivery date and time are guaranteed. If the package arrives late, you can recoup your shipping costs. Always *insure* shipments.

Careful packaging is important. No one wants their dolls or bears damaged. We recommend double boxing all shipments using corrugated cardboard boxes. There are several methods of securing fragile dolls for shipping. The best method fixes the doll in one position within a box. After wrapping the head and each arm and leg in bubble wrap, secure the doll into the box with ties around the doll's ankles, waist, and neck. Each tie passes through two slits in the bottom of the box. These slits must be carefully positioned so as not to cause stress on the doll. This box is then sealed and put into an outer shipping box which can either fit like a sleeve over the first box or be larger than the inner box, with polystyrene *peanuts* filling the void between the two boxes.

Shipping and packaging costs are among the hidden costs of your business. Most doll and teddy bear artists pass packaging and shipping costs to customers. You can set a price per doll or bear, or charge the actual shipping cost. The doll or bear can be shipped COD (collect on delivery). The customer will then have to pay the shipping charge in order to receive the box. The COD charge can include the cost of the bear or doll in addition to the cost of shipping. In this case, the shipper is responsible for paying you for the cost of the doll or bear.

Be sure your dolls or bears are insured for the retail price, regardless of what shipping method you choose. This way, if your creation is damaged during shipping, you will be reimbursed. If this happens, make sure you and your customer discuss how this will be handled as soon as possible.

CHAPTER TWELVE

Sales Booths

*S*elling at shows is the most popular sales method for doll and teddy bear artists. In chapter 14, we give you tips on selling at retail and wholesale shows. In this chapter, we concentrate on how to design your sales booth for maximum sales.

Your sales booth is your window of opportunity to attract buyers. And it's a very small window! You have less than five seconds to draw the attention of each person walking by your booth. Go back to your research. Remember when we told you to attend shows and look at ways other artists presented their work? Did you take mental or written notes? What drew you to certain booths? Why were you not drawn to others? Think about the details. Know what appeals to you.

YOUR PERSONAL STYLE

Your personal style must come through in everything you do for your business. This means that everything you do visually to promote your work should have a common thread—your magazine advertisements, your direct-mail pieces, your sales booth. You will never give justice to your work if you merely stand or sit each doll and teddy bear on the table top. And you will not attract buyers. Your display is your presentation, and you want to present your work in the most appealing way possible.

Before you dig through your personal possessions or rush out to make a substantial investment, look at yourself, your home, your surroundings, the things you love and your work. What do you see? Is there a common thread? What would people learn about you if they were viewing these things without ever speaking to or meeting you? Would they see a lover of the Victorian era? A bright French country look? A crisp art-deco image? A rustic Americana warmth? You will be most comfortable and your work will look its best if you use a decor or theme close to your own heart.

Monika uses a consistently elegant presentation. She only shows four to six dolls at a time, using black table covers draped with matching fringed crocheted shawls or table covers. She uses a three-way black display board behind each doll. These display boards come in either cardboard or foam core board and are already in a three-way configuration, available at office supply stores. Each doll is placed on a black riser in front of the three-way display board. Between each backdrop and doll, Monika places a tall, silk floral arrangement in a glass vase. Not only is this an elegant presentation for Monika's dolls, it is her signature look. Dealers and collectors know at a glance that it is her booth.

Sandy Dineen's teddies wear soft vintage clothing, and so does Sandy. Her presentation also incorporates a soft, vintage feeling. We can picture Sandy's home without ever having been there! Her consistent presentation has enhanced her sales potential.

Soft-sculpture doll artist Belinda Barry has the wonderful ability to project herself in her entire presentation. She lives in a Victorian home, and she transports aspects of her home to shows.

Teddy bear artist Debbie Lane became bored with her display but didn't want to invest in a whole new look. Barb knows Debbie like her own daughter, which made for an easy recommendation. Barb told her to spray paint her natural wood backdrop and shelving in a color she liked, perhaps burgundy, and add several six-foot-long garlands of silk roses in a lighter color and some tiny white lights for accent. Voilà! Debbie's booth had a new look. It was fresh, with lighter colors, and reflected her personality. She had wonderful sales! Sometimes we need to refresh ourselves and how we view our own displays. It's not good to become bored with our show surroundings.

MAKING THE MOST OF SPACE

Creating a winning sales booth begins with knowing how much space you have for transporting your product and setting up your materials. Will you be driving to every show? How much can you pack into your vehicle? Will you be flying? Will you carry your dolls or bears with you, or will you ship them?

Shows vary in the amount of space and type of displays available. Some shows allow shelving. Some do not permit displays more than four feet above table height. Some do not allow you to bring your own tables or shelving. Learn what is permitted at the show at which you plan to exhibit before you invest in displays you cannot use.

You will have at least one table, about $6' \times 8'$ long. Some shows will give you wall space or shelf space, but if you have a basic setup on a 6' × 8' table, you will be able to adjust it to meet requirements of specific shows. Tabletops are usually 30" deep, although those provided by production companies are frequently 24" deep. Be sure to ask if tables are provided if this information is not on the show contract.

Begin by setting up your display at home. If you don't have a dining room or kitchen table 6' × 8' long, there are other options. One is purchasing a folding table at an off-price office supply store. Sturdy 8' tables cost about forty dollars. Once you have one, you will be amazed that you ever lived without one, two or three. Don't laugh. Barb's logic in buying so many was that they could be used at shows and in her studio—which is exactly where they go!

Once you have a table, practice arranging your merchandise so all people at all eye levels can appreciate your work. Most new artists overlook the average height of the public. If you're 5'11" tall, you don't think of the segment of the population that's only 5'2". The opposite is also true. People see things at eye level, or just below eye level, first. Of course, your customers at shows have eye levels ranging from table height for those in wheelchairs to just under six feet. How can you possibly arrange your work so it can be seen at all these eye levels? It's not an impossible task, we promise!

You can make display risers that will allow your work to be shown at a variety of eye levels. Jacques Dorier has made such risers out of poster-board taped together to form boxes that fold flat. His work is lightweight enough to stand on the boxes. He's the envy of every doll artist because he carries not only his display but also his dolls into a show in one trip! Jacques moves his dolls to the eye level of collectors and buyers. Teddy bear artist Carolyn Lamothe and teddy bear shop owner Marjorie Speck of Country Bear use wonderful old wooden crates and timeworn boards in their display presentations. These crates reflect the old, country image they are trying to portray and allow their bears to be noticeable to people of all heights. Barb occasionally uses risers made of wood that extend the length of each table and add a great deal to her presentation. Whatever method you choose, varying the levels at which your dolls are shown will enhance your presentation.

If you prefer a booth space in which customers can walk into your area, consider purchasing a carpet. These can create an inviting, home-like atmosphere. This is purely a matter of taste, preference and available transportation space.

MAKING RISERS FOR YOUR DISPLAY
MATERIAL LIST
- Pine boards (2) $1'' \times 10'' \times 8'$
- Pine board (1) $1'' \times 10'' \times 6'$
- "L" brackets (8)
- Screws (16-32) $\frac{3}{4}''$

If you want to fit as much as you can onto an $8'$ table without overcrowding make risers like Barb's. Use the following directions to make a $1'$ riser and a $2'$ riser. Buy two $1'' \times 10'' \times 8'$ pine boards at a lumber shop. These $8'$ boards will become your two shelf tops. Buy one $1'' \times 10'' \times 6'$ board, and cut it into two $1'$ sections and two $2'$ sections. These cut boards will be the legs for your risers. Buy eight L brackets at a hardware store along with sixteen $\frac{3}{4}''$ screws. Buy an extra set of sixteen screws to use as spares! Each L bracket will have two holes in either end of the L. Secure two of these brackets, using the screws, to one end of each leg, about $6''$ to $8''$ apart. Lay one of the $8'$ boards on the floor. Position each $1'$ leg so that the attached L brackets are $1'$ in from each end of the $8'$ board. Attach the legs to the $8'$ board, using screws through the L brackets. Attach the $2'$ legs to the other $8'$ board in the same manner.

Stand your risers up with the taller one in back. Put them right next to one another. When placed along the rear edge of a normal-sized $8' \times 30''$ tabletop, you will have a stepped effect. You can paint or stain the boards, so you can use them without covering them if they fit your presentation. You can cover them to match or contrast with your table cover fabric.

One benefit to using this display is that it creates a hidden work space on your table. You have plenty of storage space for the cash box, receipts, credit card forms, and extra stock under the stepped shelving. If you use a drape to cover the shelving, you can bring the drape down over the back side (sheets work wonderfully). This adds a visual barrier to the things you want to protect at shows.

If your work is more than $24''$ tall, use only one riser with $2'$ legs as a rear riser on a tabletop. Stagger the height of the dolls and teddy bears you place directly on the tabletop by using individual risers about $6''$ to $7''$ high for every other doll or teddy bear.

TABLE COVERS

Many cities and towns have fire codes regulating table covers. Some require fire-retardant table covers. This doesn't mean you have to rent or purchase special table covers. Your local fire department can tell you where to purchase a fire retardant spray to apply yourself. You may buy such a spray from mail-order companies specializing in exhibit setups and materials. Fire-retardant fabric will not support flames. The flames extinguish themselves. Many 100 percent polyester fabrics behave this way.

One couple we know has exhibited their work at side-by-side booth spaces for years. They purchased three cans of fire-retardant spray years ago and set them out on their booth tables during setup. The inspectors walked right by their booth each time. We also know of shows where inspectors do the match test at every booth. That vintage table cover just might not work at some locations.

Sheets make great table covers if you buy the nonwrinkle kind! They are easy to fold, easy to wash, and they come in a wide range of colors. No-iron table covers also work well. Be sure to check the measurements to ensure they will cover the tables!

Some artists use an accent fabric over basic table covers. This can be anything you choose. Barb has several long lengths of lace which she uses to bring brightness to the display when she feels it's necessary. Another artist who loves the vintage look uses lengths of a lightweight drapery fabric with a moiré appearance. Others specializing in a Christmas theme use holiday table covers. Use only those table covers or accent fabrics that will not distract from your product.

USING DISPLAY-ONLY ITEMS

Every artist has a story about some display-only item collectors try to buy. Teddy bear artist Pat Wright-Buckley incorporates antiques into her display. She has encountered determined collectors intent on buying her display items! Despite this problem, incorporating display-only items enhances your presentation.

Are you a basket collector? It's easy to incorporate baskets into teddy bear displays. Old luggage that draws the collector's mind to another era creates an appealing aura for your dolls or teddy bears. These can also be used to transport your work.

Sonja Violette of Miss Addie's Attic uses a custom-made mirror as the focus for her displays. The mirror looks like part of a fireplace mantle in an elegant old home.

LIGHTING

One contrast between doll and teddy bear displays is the use of lighting. Doll artists frequently use lighting, while few teddy bear artists do. The lighting used in exhibit halls and hotel ballrooms often causes color changes. Some fabrics and wig colors look awful under certain lighting conditions.

Halogen bulbs give the most natural light, but can be expensive. Companies specializing in displays and exhibits offer wonderful tiny light fixtures that stand on their own or clip onto display boards. They are costly but appealing.

Halogen lighting doesn't have to be a major investment. Large hardware stores and specialty lighting shops carry screw-in halogen bulbs that can convert regular lighting units into halogen lights. Ask if you can test one in a lamp or if you can exchange the bulb if it doesn't give the coverage you need. Spotlights and floodlights do two entirely different things. Sylvania makes two varieties of each. What you need depends on the effect and coverage you want.

When buying lamps, remember that you will be transporting them. You don't need a fragile lamp to break during transport or setup. Barb has two readily available floor units with three adjustable lamp heads on each one. They have a heavy, weighted base ensuring they won't tip easily. Each is 60″ tall and can be positioned on the floor or on the tabletop. These lamps are available at discount stores on sale for about twenty dollars each. One fixture gives excellent coverage to an eight foot table.

Barb has half a dozen small accent lamps with adjustable angles. These come in black, white, bright brass and chrome finishes and cost under fifteen dollars each. All these lamps and bulbs and extra extension cords store and transport neatly in a large plastic tote with a hinged lid.

It can be terribly disappointing to travel to a show and have nothing sell because the lighting alters the color of your teddy bears or washes out your doll's complexion. This is something we can control. Good lighting has helped make a sell-out presentation at shows for more than one artist. Don't use the excuse, "The lighting ruined my display!" This is your business and you are in charge.

SALES TOOLS

Your booth would not be complete without business tools to enhance sales—both at the show and after you pack up and go home. The following list covers the basic types of tools you need.

- Business cards. These are an absolute must—the easiest way for a collector to contact you after the show. Business cards are cheap and easy to acquire. Don't forget them!
- Clearly visible pricing. Can pricing be a selling tool? Yes. Many collectors will not look at a price tag, believing the price will be too high. Remember, we all see prices listed on the shelf below items at the grocery store and at many other retail businesses. Price is one of the four factors affecting purchasing decisions. Many artists use small tent cards (heavy paper folded in half with the name, edition size and price) or small photo frames beside each doll or teddy to clearly show the price of each piece.
- Awards. If your teddy bear or doll has received a nomination or won an award, show it off. Put it in a frame and place it next to the doll or bear.
- Flyers about you and your work. These can range from photocopied sheets to elaborate brochures to catalogs. See chapter 11 for more information about sales literature, flyers and brochures.
- Guest books. Do you use a guest book? This is a great way to add to your mailing list. Collectors don't always have bottomless pockets. If they take the time to sign your guest book, they like your work.
- A list of upcoming shows. Put out flyers listing the dates and locations of upcoming shows in which you will participate. These don't have to be full-page flyers. One-half, one-third or one-quarter page flyers achieve the same results. Size depends on the length of your list.

WHERE IS YOUR PORTFOLIO?

Forget about modesty. People buying your dolls and bears may not know you sell at every show. Perhaps they didn't see the four-page article about you in that doll or teddy bear magazine a year ago. Maybe they weren't collecting then!

Your portfolio is more than a brag book. A well-prepared portfolio is an inviting textbook for collectors and retailers. Start with photos of how your work progresses. The public is entranced by how we create our dolls and bears. A series of photos showing pattern design, cutting the mohair, unstuffed teddies, teddies with no faces, and the final creation, will interest newer collectors. You will have on hand a graphic reply to the question "Where did you get those heads?" Show your dolls from the earliest stages of creation (sketches and armature) to the finished product. Include photos of mold making if you make your own plaster or latex molds.

Add every magazine article, newspaper article and photo of or about you and your work to your portfolio, as well as any nominations or awards you've received. Advertisements can also be included. For information on how to cut and paste newspaper articles, see chapter 8.

People buy into success or perceived success. Your portfolio presents your success as an artist to everyone who looks at it. Place your portfolio where collectors and shop owners can see it at every show.

TIPS FOR SETTING UP AND TEARING DOWN

Whatever you use to enhance your presentation, practice setting up your display before going to the show. Time yourself. Know what you will need first, and pack it so it's the first thing you unload. Identify each container to avoid the frustration of finding what you need in the last box. This makes for easier breaking down at the end of the show. Organized artists have time to check out other exhibits and visit with friends during setup time. They can break down a display quickly and get back on the road following shows first.

CHAPTER THIRTEEN

Selling at Shows

*S*hows are the most popular places for doll and teddy bear artists to sell their creations. There are distinct differences between wholesale and retail shows. We suggest you gain experiences exhibiting and selling at retail shows before investing in booth space at larger, more expensive wholesale shows. We will discuss retail shows first. At the end of this chapter, we will give you basic information about selling at wholesale shows. If you are interested in more specific information about sales contracts and the other business aspects of selling wholesale, read chapter 14.

WHY DO A RETAIL SHOW?

Sales are your primary reason for exhibiting at shows. Don't give up after poor sales at just one show. There are many hidden benefits to doing a show.

Retail shows boost name-recognition. Collectors eagerly await retail shows. Some plan vacations around certain shows. The collectors are there because they intend to buy! Never will you be able to meet so many eager collectors face-to-face. Many of them may have never heard of you, but you will have the chance to impress them. They can see your work in person. They will take home one of your business cards. If they see you at more than one show, they will begin to recognize your name and your presentation style. This leads to future sales.

Shows and conventions are good places to practice the skills we discussed in earlier chapters. Remember the importance of networking and research? At retail shows you'll meet other artists, get feedback and learn new things about your craft. Here your competitors can become your friends. Walk around. Talk to other exhibitors. Networking and research are lifelong skills.

Remember that lecture or program you developed to promote yourself? Will it interest collectors or other artists? If so, consider presenting it at a show. Don't wait to be asked. Ask the organizer if he needs a presenter. Send him materials about your presentation.

Many shows and conventions include contests. In chapter 6, we discussed how entering can enhance name recognition. Consider entering one of your dolls or bears.

CHOOSING THE RIGHT SHOWS

Retail shows may be produced by individual collectors or artists, doll or teddy bear clubs or large production companies. Some last a few hours. Others last several days and include programs, workshops and similar events. No type of show is better than any other, but they vary in number of exhibitors, attendance and range of items shown. *The Doll Sourcebook* and *The Teddy Bear Sourcebook*, both published by Betterway Books, contain comprehensive listings for many shows. Doll and teddy bear magazines list shows and include contact people who can give you more information.

If you cannot attend a show before exhibiting, ask for information to help you decide if the show is right for you. Besides the general questions, such as space available, cost, and time to report for setup, consider how your dolls and bears will fit with the others in terms of style and price range. Think about how many people attend, and if they are your "type" of buyers. Consider how the show is promoted. The promoter or organizer should be happy to answer your questions. Ask her for names of artists who have exhibited at the show. Get the artists' point of view by asking them the same questions.

The hardest part of this research is learning about the buying habits of collectors likely to attend. This varies year to year, and different artists will have different viewpoints depending on how well they have done at a given show in the past. Talk to more than one person. A California artist who exhibits at East Coast shows told us about a New York promoter who organizes several shows. One of the show locations attracts collectors who want to see an artist at three or four shows before they start buying from her. Another location attracts just the opposite—buyers seem to be looking for something new, and first-time exhibitors tend to do well. Shows at different locations by the same promoter do not always attract the same type of buyer!

If you are a newer artist, begin with smaller shows. You will build name

FINDING OUT DETAILS OF A SHOW

Before you attend a show, ask the promoter or organizer as well as previous exhibitors the following questions:

- How many exhibitors attend?
- How many are selling original dolls or teddy bears? Will there be a mixture of old and new, manufactured, reproductions and artist originals?
- Is this a "mixed" show where dolls or bears are only one type of item that will be sold?
- In what price range are most of the dolls or bears?
- How many people usually attend?
- Are most of the collectors in attendance from the local or regional area? If not, how far do they travel?
- What are the buying habits of collectors attending these shows? Do first-time exhibitors generally do well?
- How is this show advertised? Will your name be included in the advertisements?
- Does the show have a mailing list? If so, how many people are included?

recognition and gain valuable experience, allowing you to fix errors in your presentation before exhibiting at a larger, more popular show.

MORE TIPS FOR BETTER SALES

Review chapter 5 on marketing yourself along with your bears and chapter 12 on sales booths. These chapters will be invaluable in terms of sales. Say your display is impeccable, and the show seems right for you in terms of the price ranges and types of items being sold. You are talking to customers, putting your best foot forward. You know your product is the best it can be. You feel you are doing everything right, but sales are lagging. What do you do?

One trick of the trade is to pay attention to the collector's eye. When she begins to admire a doll or teddy bear, you will want to approach her and talk to her about this special creation. As you do, if possible, put the doll or bear into her arms. Once an item is off the shelf, the collector begins to take ownership.

Dale Junker, a teddy bear supplies and accessories retailer who sells at numerous shows every year, told us an amusing story about his early days of selling teddy bears at shows. Once he'd put the teddy bear into the customer's arms, he would rearrange the space where the teddy bear had been so there was no empty place to put it back. This made the collector hold the bear longer.

Some artists change the table arrangement after two hours if the dolls or bears aren't selling. When the collector goes by again, she will think the artist's dolls or bears are selling, and will take another look!

ACCEPTING PAYMENT

Selling dolls and bears means being paid in some manner—preferably a negotiable instrument like money! A negotiable instrument is anything regularly and routinely accepted in exchange for currency.

There are always pros (benefits) to being paid. Unfortunately, there are also cons to consider, and those negatives always seem to be in one category: worthless instruments such as rubber checks, or credit card charges on which we didn't get authorization until after we gave the merchandise to the customer and after the customer was no longer in our presence.

CASH

Accepting only cash means you could be carrying a large sum of money. See, we're confident that you can have a very successful show! It's not terribly difficult to notice which exhibitors have successful shows, and who is taking in large sums of cash.

On the pro side, there are several tools available to determine the authenticity of U.S. dollars. (We're qualifying this because we have no idea if these same tools work on foreign currency.) There's a pen resembling a felt-tip marker that's available for under five dollars. You mark questionable bills with the pen. One color indicates the bill is legitimate, another color indicates it's counterfeit. There is also a lighted tool which costs more than the pens do. You place questionable bills under the light.

You don't have to wait for cash to clear your bank. It is accepted everywhere—unlike second-party checks. Cash is an immediately negotiable instrument. Many people believe accepting only cash restricts their business. I'm sure you've heard collectors ask if you accept checks or credit cards. Most artists do accept checks.

CREDIT CARDS

Accepting credit cards is an added business expense. We must caution you that having a merchant account (this means you accept credit cards) does not mean the collectors *will* charge their purchases. In some areas, it is difficult for in-home businesses to qualify for merchant accounts. There is also an initial cost of equipment and monthly charges to consider along with the fee on each charge. The fee varies according to the dollar volume of business you do (or expect to do) through the merchant account.

APPLYING FOR A MERCHANT ACCOUNT

In most cases, you can apply for a merchant account, which allows you to accept credit card purchases, through your local bank. You can also call Superior Bank Card at (800) 621-2794 for MasterCard or Visa merchant accounts, (800) 528-5200 for American Express merchant accounts, and Novus Network Services at (800) 347-6673 for Discover Card merchant accounts.

After studying the retail habits of the public, Barb believes these charges are worth incurring. During a six-week study at a retail chain store offering merchandise ranging from under a dollar to several thousand dollars, Barb found the majority of sales were paid for with credit cards (even very small purchases). Payment by check closely followed the dollar volume of credit-card purchases. Cash payments were way behind. Barb estimated the cash receipts as being no more than 15 percent of total sales.

Why does the public write checks and use so much plastic? So they don't have to carry cash. Many credit cards are debit cards. A debit card is just like a credit card to the merchant but the amount purchased is deducted from the buyer's checking account—no bills to pay. Credit card charges can be paid for at a later date, or spread over a period of time. Some credit cards have the added benefit of insuring purchases charged to the card against breakage, loss or theft. And, of course, credit cards let people make purchases they could not otherwise afford or might not make if cash were the only option at the time of purchase.

Your merchant account allows you to do credit card approvals by phone or machine. Take the time to do this. A large west coast show was hit by at least three individuals who made purchases on the last day of the show. They bought only from exhibitors who were not getting credit card approvals. From what we were able to learn, those hit by these people each had to travel at least four hours to get home. When they got home and tried for authorization on the charges, they were each denied. They were told the cards were reported stolen.

There was some sort of scam going on that day. We learned of over forty thousand dollars in charges that were made the last day of that show—

all on credit cards reported stolen the evening before or the morning of the day of the purchases. Each one of these could have been avoided if the seller had taken a few minutes to get prior approval.

Do not use a cellular phone when seeking verbal authorization on credit cards or checks. Cellular phone calls can be monitored by almost any scanner, and this is how many numbers and expiration dates fall into hands that will use them illegally.

There is nothing wrong with asking for additional identification whenever a customer presents a check or credit card. You are protecting their interests as well as yours. It has become quite common for people not to sign their credit cards. Instead, they are writing "see photo ID," "C I D," or "ask for identification" in the signature area.

CHECKS

A check is a legal contract. The writer or giver of the check is indicating he intends to pay the amount stated to the payee named on the check. You have legal recourse if these funds are not payable to you upon presentation of the check.

It is important to verify and record the identification of the person writing the check. If the check is in a company or business name, be sure you have the current address and telephone number of the company. Record the name of the person presenting the check. Write it above the printed name of the business. Record the presenter's address, telephone number, and date of birth as well as his driver's license number and issuing state. This information is necessary if the check is not negotiable.

We cannot be paranoid, thinking every person with a checkbook is trying to pass a bad check. Yet, we must protect ourselves. Here are some clues to remember:

• Don't accept postdated checks. Checks dated a day or two in the future indicates the funds are not in the account now. If the money isn't there, you don't want the check. Too many things can happen that may result in anticipated deposits not being made.

• Don't accept checks where the name in the *Pay to the Order* line has been scratched out. This indicates the check may have been stolen. Ask the customer to issue a new check.

• Don't accept checks with mismatched dollar amounts. People passing stolen checks often change the numerical dollar figure to indicate a higher amount. It is easier to change numbers than written words. Look closely at the numerical dollar amount of *$100*. Are the zeros squeezed together?

One zero may have been added after the check was stolen. Read the written descriptive amount. *This* is the amount the bank will use in paying any check. You may see *ten dollars* instead of *one hundred dollars*. Obviously, you will not accept such a check.

• Don't accept the check if the serial numbers and check numbers do not match. The numbering along the bottom of checks are printed with magnetic ink that the bank's automated processing machines use. These numbers include the bank's identification number, the account number and the last four digits, which should always be the same as the serialized number of the check in the upper right-hand corner.

• Crooks often change the number at the top of the check for two reasons. If the checks have been stolen, the bank may have already reported the serial numbers of the stolen checks to electronic check-verification services. The thief may have altered these numbers to be different from those on the stolen checks. Crooks may also alter the magnetic number to indicate an out-of-town bank location. This is to slow down the check during the clearance process, giving the thief a longer period of time to pass bad checks. In either case, you're getting a bad check. Be sure the numbers match and that they haven't been altered in any way.

• Don't accept the check if the amount is greater than the purchase price of your merchandise. This customer doesn't want your doll or teddy bear—she wants your cash. This is where the majority of bad checks occur.

• Don't accept checks that are not imprinted with the customer's name and address. Blank or starter checks may not be good. Barb even questions those with the name imprinted but no other information. Every time Barb writes a check for a purchase, they want her street address as well as the imprinted mailing address. They circle her telephone number and record her driver's license, date of birth and expiration date of the license. Many people have all of this information printed on their checks today. Other than those civic groups without a permanent mailing address or a physical location (the elected treasurer is the keeper of the checkbook), why would anyone not have at least a home address imprinted on their checks?

• Always ask for photo ID. You have no way of knowing any check belongs to the person presenting the check. A driver's license works best. Ask if the address is current. Compare the address on the check with that on the identification. Look at the photo. Compare the signature.

• Be sure the bank branch is indicated on the check. Whenever doing a show in any area, take a moment to read through the banks listed in the yellow pages of the local telephone book. This may only make you familiar with local banks, but most of your customers will probably be local people.

- Don't accept second- or third-party checks. A second-party check is one made out by a person other than the customer, payable to the customer. A company payroll check is an example. A third-party check is one made out by a person or company payable to a second person, who has in turn made it payable to the customer. Typically, such a check has been made payable to a relative of the customer. There is too big a chance the second- or third-party check is phony. You have no way of verifying signatures and you don't even have the check maker's word that the check is good.

Also, watch for these behavioral patterns:

- The overly emotional person with a hard luck story. An example is the collector you've never met before who asks you to cash a check to tide her over until the bank opens. The money machine just swallowed her card. She may be posing as a collector to get your dollars.
- The wild shopper buying as much of anything she can with no concern for prices. She may be using the merchandise as an excuse to cash a check.
- Beware of the collectors who become upset with delays caused by your security practices. Do not be intimidated if they get upset or say they are in a hurry. They are doing this so that you won't follow your established procedures!

Today, computers and laser printers are available to nearly everyone, and some people are making their own checks on banks existing only in their minds. In many states, the only place a person can be apprehended for writing a bad check is in the city or town where the check was accepted, so act quickly if someone acts suspiciously. Contact the police or a security person at the show, as well as the show organizer, immediately.

The following happened during the afternoon of the last day of a large show. A woman approached Barb saying she wanted to write a check for a doll. She offered an even-dollar amount that was neither the price on the hangtag nor the total with the correct sales tax added.

Barb said she could not accept the woman's check but could accept a credit card. The woman said she always "paid up front." Barb explained that she had no way of verifying a check but could verify a credit card. She added that credit card payments were "up front" to her.

The woman realized Barb was not about to accept a check from her and simply signed the guest book in Barb's booth and wandered off. As soon as she'd left, another artist approached Barb. She was obviously distressed. The artist asked to see "the check that woman just gave you." At first Barb didn't understand. She said she hadn't accepted a check from anyone and must have had a very puzzled expression on her face. The artist insisted she'd seen that woman signing something. Barb realized she must have meant the woman who'd just signed her guest book.

Aha! The artist recognized the woman's name as that of a woman who had given the artist a worthless check at this same show the previous year. Other artists began to gather. One suggested she find the show promoter. Barb immediately told her to contact the security guard at the door. Wasn't this why he was there? The artist contacted the security guard and fortunately a local police officer was there talking with his friend, the security officer.

The two officers followed that woman up the escalator, through the lobby and onto the elevator before the police officer was able to confront her. The woman initially denied her name was the same as the one she'd signed in Barb's guest book, but quickly admitted the truth when the officer said there was a witness who would identify her as the same person who signed that name just a few minutes before. Rumor had it the woman had passed over eight thousand dollars in bad checks at the show the year before.

To protect your check from being stolen and used by someone else, endorse every check with "For Deposit Only to the Account of Payee" as soon as you accept each check. This prevents others from depositing checks meant for you.

Take precautions to protect your cash, checks and credit card receipts. Put them all in a secure location. This can be a cash box *if* someone will be with the cash box at all times, or a wallet or waist pack that stays with you. Artists have discovered their purses have been stolen before the show closed. Take steps to protect what is yours!

CAN YOU REALLY SELL WHOLESALE AT RETAIL SHOWS?

Of course you can. You should expect to be approached by shop owners at retail shows. Not every retailer makes her purchasing decisions for the year at trade shows. Some never attend trade shows! Few teddy bear artists attend trade shows, so the teddy bear retailers only have retail shows as a venue for seeing artist-made originals. We would all like to sell every doll and teddy bear for the full retail price. There are great benefits to selling to shops, however. See chapter 14 for more information on selling wholesale.

There are two main "rules" to selling wholesale at a retail show: Be prepared, and be discreet. You must be prepared for all sorts of scenarios. Know if you will consider selling one of your creations to a shop at all, and if so, at what price. If you cannot afford the normal 30 to 50 percent discount, don't let your ego get in the way when a retailer asks. Tell the retailer your situation, and offer a smaller discount if possible.

Shop owners know you will make more money selling the doll or bear directly to collectors. Often they will say that they want certain pieces at the end of the show if you don't sell them. They may also say they will place an order if the pieces sell. If they do not offer these options, offer them yourself! When discussing cost with a retailer, be discreet. You don't want to confuse the collector who overheard you quote a wholesale price to a shop owner.

TRADE SHOWS

What makes a trade show different from a retail show? Trade shows are on the opposite end of the selling world. People attending these shows are making purchasing decisions based on what they think will make a profit for their businesses. They are trying to project what will move within their customer base.

Trade shows are not usually open to the public. A few shows allow collectors in on the last day of the show, but they cannot buy from exhibitors. Trade shows allow the artist a chance to present merchandise to shop owners and buyers for businesses which retail to the public.

At this writing, there are no trade shows featuring only teddy bears. There are, however, several venues for dolls or dolls and teddy bears. Some of these include the International Toy Fair sponsored each February in New York City by the Toy Manufacturers of America, and the International Doll Expo held each January in the U.S. There are also several established shows throughout Europe. Some artists have found success exhibiting at gift market trade shows in the U.S. and Europe.

Exhibiting at trade shows (wholesale shows) is expensive. The cost of presenting these shows is high, and this cost is passed on to exhibitors so the promoter can make a profit. For this reason, carefully weigh the pros and cons of participating in such a show, and consider your goals and experience as an artist. Unless you have been selling widely at retail shows and by mail, jumping into a trade show is not a good idea.

The comment we hear most frequently from first-time trade-show exhibitors is "It's so strange not to have people oohing and aahing over my work! They just look and buy with no emotion." The wholesale buyer is making business decisions. He is buying your products because he believes they will sell in his shops.

Before selling at a trade show, have a sales contract available for each customer and have all your sales policies spelled out. Carefully consider your wholesale prices for specific dolls. Chapter 14 will help you establish business policies for wholesale sales.

CHAPTER FOURTEEN

Selling Wholesale

*S*elling wholesale means selling to someone who is going to resell your doll or teddy bear to someone else. For doll and teddy bear artists, it usually means selling to a doll, teddy bear, collectible toy or fine art and craft shop. We have already touched on wholesale sales in chapters 11 and 13, when we discussed how to attract the attention of shop owners via mail order and at retail and wholesale shows. This chapter will give you detailed advice on establishing sales policies.

DISADVANTAGES TO SELLING WHOLESALE

Logic says that the retailer has to make a profit, and must price your work accordingly. Herein lies the problem for many artists. Some artists believe that the suggested retail price—generally the price the artists themselves charge collectors—should be set by the artist and no retailer should ever deviate from that retail price. Sorry, but this is price fixing and is an illegal practice in the U.S. When selling wholesale, you have control of the price you charge the retailer, but not the final price for which the bear or doll is sold. This is the major disadvantage of selling wholesale.

Think of it this way: Each of us has the right to sell any item we own at whatever price we choose. A business needs cash flow to stay in business. Every retail business has sales at some time. The word *sale* indicates that the price is reduced from the normal price. A product costs a retailer money if it doesn't sell within forty-five days (and this is stretching it in some industries). Shops need cash flow to buy new merchandise.

We believe that each of us must be happy with whatever price we choose to accept for a doll or teddy bear. After all, the price we get is all we get and therefore the only price with which we have to be concerned. Set aside emotional attachment to your work. Set aside your ego. Step back and look at this from a logical perspective. Consider these facts:

- The artist has created the sculpture or design through individual creative talents.
- The artist has invested time and materials.
- The artist bears the cost of doing business.
- The artist must profit beyond actual expenses to make money.

Now, consider these facts:

- Retailers present their merchandise to collectors in shops which have overhead expenses, at shows which have costs with which we are familiar, and through advertising.
- Like the artist, the retailer has a financial investment in each doll and teddy bear. And, like the artist, the retailer does not recoup his or her investment until the item is sold.

Occasionally we hear artists complain that the retailer is making 50 percent of the retail price with no investment. This is especially common when a retailer frequently buys from one artist and doesn't advertise that artist's dolls or teddies. If they can sell without the cost of advertising, so much the better for both the retailer and the collector. If a doll or teddy bear sells quickly and without further investment, the retailer will come back to the artist for more. That artist's work is profitable for the retailer. Everyone profits, and isn't that the bottom line?

There are retailers who show photographs of dolls or bears to collectors and then place orders with the artist after securing an order from a collector. Some artists feel that in these cases, the artist is making a greater investment than the retailer, who does not even have to find a spot in her shop for the doll or bear. The bottom line is what matters. The artist is selling her work to someone who otherwise may have never seen it. Shop owners do not have bottomless pockets any more than we do.

If you are going to sell wholesale, you are going to encounter these situations. Don't dwell on the negative. It affects your work. You must be happy with whatever price you charge for your doll or teddy bear. Period. If you are not happy, you have no one to blame but yourself because you are the one who set that price.

ADVANTAGES TO SELLING WHOLESALE

There are many reasons to sell wholesale. By doing so, you are able to reach segments of the collector population you might otherwise not reach. For instance, you may choose to sell in shops far from home. If you cannot afford to travel to shows in these locations, this may be the only way collectors will have the chance to see and touch your bears in person. Many collectors will not buy via mail order if they have not seen the bears in person first.

By selling your creations to shops, you allow the shop owner to take some advertising and promotion pressure off you. The shop owner now has as much of an investment in your doll or bear as you. She wants to sell that doll or bear. She's going to display it in a way that shows it off. She's going to talk about you with collectors who enter her shop. Your name will be on the lips of people who may never have met you!

Many shops have a featured-artist section in which the work of one artist is displayed for a specific period of time. Ask the shop owners if they do this type of promotion. Perhaps they never considered using this merchandising technique!

Shops schedule artist signings which are advertised in magazines and local media. These events can include a single artist or a group of artists and are scheduled well in advance. The advance scheduling allows the artists time to create merchandise for the event. Some artists require the retailer to purchase a given number of pieces or a minimum dollar amount. Most allow artists to bring additional dolls and teddy bears. If these are sold during the artist's visit, the retailer gets a lower percentage of the retail price, often only 20 percent. If the artist's work sells well, the shop owners often purchase unsold pieces the artist brought along.

It is not uncommon for the retailer to provide lodging for signings and gallery shows. Some even offer travel expenses. Others schedule workshops and classes in sculpting or teddy bear making in conjunction with these events. Workshops are a great way to make extra money when traveling to other areas of the country—especially to shops offering your work!

Gallery shows are another way shops promote a group of artists. These, too, are well advertised. The terms and conditions of sales vary widely from gallery showing to gallery showing. Be sure you know and understand the terms before you agree to participate.

Gallery shows allot each artist a predetermined amount of display space. The artist does not get a full retail price for any piece sold. A percentage goes to the person organizing the event. When is the artist paid for his portion of sales? This is an important question.

Expenses to attend a signing or gallery show are business expenses. Do costs to participate compare to the monies derived from potential sales of the pieces you will exhibit? It is easy to let our egos rule our decisions to participate in different events, but egos don't pay the bills. Many talented artists have been forced to stop making their wonderful creations because expenses outweighed income.

You control how you want to sell your creations. You control your financial resources. Do not be afraid to make business decisions that meet your needs. If you have to decline an opportunity, simply say that it doesn't fit your schedule and/or budget for that year. But be sure to thank the person for the opportunity and indicate that you are interested in future signings or gallery shows.

SALES POLICIES

Work on your sales policies for wholesale sales now. Even if you don't expect to sell wholesale, you may be approached by a retailer at a show. It's best to know where you stand in terms of policies and to have a sales contract ready.

Why do we use the words *sales policies* instead of *policy*? Because you should have different terms for one-of-a-kind dolls and teddy bears and limited editions. Why? Usually, the one-of-a-kind doll or bear has already been completed. Delayed shipments will lead to the buyer changing her mind. The shop owner knows she wants a piece when she sees it. She knows if it is within her budget. There is no reason to delay payment in full to you beyond thirty days from the date the shop owner tells you she wants to purchase the doll or bear. Likewise, you should ship the product as soon as the shop's check has cleared your bank.

Many wholesale sales will be made through contacts at trade or retail shows. Because of this, you must clearly communicate what you are open to selling wholesale when exhibiting at shows. For instance, once you place a "sold" sign on a doll or teddy, you have told other potential buyers it isn't available. If sold tags are put on dolls and bears that are part of an edition, and the edition is not sold out, write a note saying that you will accept orders for other dolls and bears in that edition right on your sold tag!

Will you accept backup orders? A backup order is an order for a one-of-a-kind bear or doll or an edition that has already been sold out. In this scenario, a retailer can put his name on a waiting list—if the first buyer does not complete the purchase, the next buyer has the option to buy.

Another sales policy that has worked for several artists is a way to encourage shop owners to arrange for timely delivery dates and multiple purchases. The closer the delivery date is to the date of sale, the lower the price. The further the delivery date is to the date of sale, the greater the wholesale cost. For example:

- Wholesale orders must be for a minimum of three dolls.
- A 15 percent discount for deliveries scheduled within thirty days of the order.
- A 10 percent discount for deliveries scheduled within thirty to sixty days of the order.
- Full retail price for deliveries sixty to ninety days from the date of the order.
- No orders accepted after ninety days.

Another example:

- One-of-a-kind dolls must be paid in full within fourteen days from the date of order, with shipment after the check has cleared the artist's bank.
- Delivery after payment has cleared the artist's bank, with shipping charges COD, payable to shipper.
- For limited editions sold to retailers, one doll at full retail price, two dolls at 35 percent off retail price, three or more dolls at 50 percent off retail price. All payments must be received within thirty days of order. Doll will be shipped when the check has cleared the artist's bank.

You are the one making and offering your creations to shop owners, so the sales should be on your terms!

SALES CONTRACTS

Why on earth would you need a sales contract? Written communication can be recalled with far greater accuracy than verbal communication. When you sell a doll or teddy bear right off the table at a show, that's a direct sale. All parties know who is paying how much and for what. When you accept an order for later delivery, either at a show or over the phone, which is usually the case when you are selling to retailers, everyone involved must clearly understand and agree to the terms of the sales contract. This is also the case when accepting a retail order for future delivery.

Relax. Writing up a sales contract is not a complicated process. Several successful artists have been doing this for a long time. Here are the elements to include in every contract:

- Date of sale
- Location of sale
- Name of the buyer
- Name of the shop or business purchasing the doll, bear or edition

- Name of individual doll, bear or edition to be sold
- A complete description of each doll, bear or edition
- Number of dolls or bears in the edition
- Name of the artist and company selling the doll, bear or edition
- The wholesale price of each doll or bear
- The amount of deposit paid by the shop owner (This should be about 20 to 25 percent of the total wholesale price.)
- Date by which balance must be paid
- Method(s) of payment acceptable
- What will happen if payment is not received (Generally, you will want to put in writing that if the order is canceled, all monies paid must be forfeited.)
- When doll(s) or bear(s) will be shipped (It is best to wait until the retailer has paid in full.)
- Method of shipment (You decide how you want your work to be shipped.)
- How shipping will be paid (If you only ship with shipping charges paid COD by the buyer, you must state this on the sales contract.)
- Any special limitations on this sale (For instance, if you do not want this retailer to sell your dolls or bears to another retailer, you must specify this in the contract.)

LAYAWAY AGREEMENTS

If you accept layaway, either with individual collectors or with retailers, you should have a written contract for this as well. Do not leave anything to memory! There are far too many stories of canceled orders or misunderstandings between artists and shop owners to ignore this simple step in ensuring clear communications.

Why should a buyer pay a nonrefundable, nontransferable deposit? Because you, the artist, are filling a special order. You are paying for the materials to make each doll and teddy bear. You are also committing that doll or bear to fill a specific order. Do not be afraid to follow the sound business practices followed in every other business in which custom-made orders are placed and filled. Even automobile dealerships require a deposit when a customer places an order!

This contract protects the buyer as well as the seller. If you cannot fill the order on time, you must return all monies, including the nonrefundable deposit. Why? Because you failed to maintain your part of the sales agreement.

Be well aware of the time you will need to fill each order. Do not

SALES AGREEMENT

Date: February_____, 1996   Jacob Javits Center New York City, NY

This agreement is between Barb Giguere/*Memories & Smiles* . . . and
_____ of _____. For the
purchase of the following one-of-a-kind artist made original pieces:

_____ Allison Rose & Baby Cyril. Cernit dolls. Each doll wears artist
designed and artist made clothing. Allison's Global wig is of
modacrylic fibers. Cyril's wig is mohair. Allison has Hand glass
eyes, Cyril has *Real Eyes*. The pair is on the cover of *The Doll
Sourcebook*, due to be released November 1996.

Wholesale price $600

_____ Valerie and her Teddy. Cernit doll, Teddy of synthetic plush
by Dani Alexandre. Mohair wig by Global, *Real Eyes*, artist
made clothing.

Wholesale price $600

_____ Jannell. Cernit doll, Global modacrylic wig, *Real Eyes*, antique
shoes, artist designed/made clothing is from vintage fabrics.

Wholesale price $600

_____ Adrienne. Cernit, artist made sheepskin wig, *Real Eyes*, antique
shoes and artist designed/made clothing is from vintage fabrics.

Wholesale price $600

_____ Adrienne & Jannell. Purchased together at the same time.

Special price $1100

Total wholesale price   _____
25% non-refundable, non-transferable deposit   _____
Balance due no later than March 15, 1996   _____
Paid with _____ Cash, MC/Visa, check #   _____

Payment must be in US funds. Any final payment not received by March 15, 1996 will
result in forfeiture of 25% of the agreed purchase price and forfeiture of the product(s).
All deposits are non-refundable and non-transferable. Merchandise will be shipped via
2-day Economy FedEX, shipping charges collect to FedEX.

No molds nor mass produced dolls/bears will be made of these one-of-a-kind pieces.
Each piece is signed by the artist. A certificate of authenticity will accompany each doll/
bear.

I agree to the terms and conditions herein _____
on February _____, 1996.

Sample sales agreement

overcommit yourself. One of the quickest ways to alienate shop owners is by not meeting deadlines and delivery commitments.

Unless you are well established, do not accept orders for delivery later than ninety days from the order. Number one, interest in the bear or doll fades quickly after ninety days. Number two, you are in business to make money and your own creative directions change. You don't want to be doing the same thing a year from now that you are doing today. If a shop owner wants delivery in six months, explain that you will send them photos of your new work four months from now as you don't accept orders with delivery dates more than ninety days in advance. If he questions your business judgment, explain that it is in the shop's best interest to carry current merchandise. This isn't a rule, only a word of advice.

SPECIAL EDITIONS FOR SHOPS

Both of us are strong believers in doing exclusive editions for shops. Often this requires involving the shop owner in the creative process. "Can you make that bear in a sparse mohair dyed to match my favorite color?" is not an uncommon request. Or, "I adore that doll. She reminds me of my favorite playmate when we were children. But she had brunette hair and hazel eyes. Can you do ten of the edition like this for my shop?"

Of course, you don't have to agree to any request. But it is certainly good business to consider the request. With any of these requests, you must assess the costs of producing the dolls or bears, availability of materials, and the costs to alter your production schedule to fit the required delivery dates before you negotiate a price. Also, will the shop owner advertise the exclusive edition? If so, be sure you get a photograph to the shop owner as soon as the first doll or teddy bear in the exclusive edition is completed.

Exclusive editions make good sense for the artist *and* the shop owners. The artist knows each piece in the edition is sold. There is no speculative work. The retailer knows her shop is the only place collectors can purchase that doll or bear.

Although this is not the norm (we hope!), a few artists have made exclusive editions for shops, and then sold the same dolls or bears themselves! This is dishonest, and is not fair to the shop owner. Shop owners and collectors should have documentation from the artist stating that the edition is exclusive to a named shop.

In fact, some artists even include the name of the retail shop in the Certificate of Authenticity included with each doll and bear, on the sewn-in tag or on the hangtag. Yes, this is a bit of extra work, but it also documents the source of each doll and bear.

LAY-A-WAY AGREEMENT

Date: _____

This agreement is between artist, Barb Giguere, and customer,

_____

of _____

and is made this date at _____

Customer agrees to purchase _____

for a total purchase price of $ _____

with a 20% down payment of _____

Payments of _____ will be made _____

It is fully understood by both parties that the initial down payment is non-refundable and non-transferable. The purchaser agrees to make all payment on time, payable in U.S. funds drawn on a U.S. bank by cash, check, money order or VISA or MasterCard. Further, the customer understands that the artist will not send monthly bills nor reminders that payment is due. It is the sole responsibility of the customer to submit payments as herein agreed. If payments are not received as agreed, all monies paid are forfeited.

Doll/bear will be shipped on the business day after final payment has cleared artist's bank. Shipment will be via FedEX Economy, shipping charges COD and Payable to FedEX.

_____ _____
ARTIST   DATE   CUSTOMER   DATE

Sample layaway agreement

Don't be afraid of wholesale sales. They can open a whole new collector base to you. Selling your doll or bear in a shop in a faraway location will help you reach collectors who would not normally see your work. If you have packaged your product properly, collectors who have never met you at shows will have your address handy, and may later decide to place an order with you for another doll or bear! Selling in shops in your hometown is a good sales practice as well. Your local doll or teddy bear shop owner could become your best friend, helping you develop new ideas, critiquing your work, and recommending your dolls or bears to local collectors!

CHAPTER FIFTEEN

Going Commercial

*H*ave you ever turned on the TV and seen a teddy bear or doll being sold on a home shopping channel and wished it were yours? Have you ever received an advertisement in the mail from one of the mints with a doll or bear in it no nicer than yours, and wondered how the people who made them were ever lucky enough to have their work manufactured?

Having your designs produced by a manufacturer involves knowing the right people, knowing the market, persistence, and luck. Add talent, too—it's important, but without the other elements, talent alone will get you nowhere.

THE PROS AND CONS

Do you really want to go commercial? You have to decide for yourself if designing for a manufacturer fits your lifestyle and goals. Some artists consider selling designs to manufacturers to be selling out. You may have heard that collectors will be confused when commercial versions of your work go on the market, and that they may not want to pay the higher prices for your originals. Some people will say you are ruining the field for others, providing collectors with the "quick fix" they need, which in turn prevents them from purchasing original-artist dolls and bears.

Also, be aware: Your work will seldom look like the prototypes you make for the manufacturer. You have to learn to live with this. Your philosophy must be to take the money and run. It sounds awful, but it's true. If you can't compromise on quality, don't even consider going commercial.

You must also be prepared to work on deadline and remake your doll or bear many times before it is acceptable as a prototype for the manufacturer. You also must have patience. It can take up to two years from the time you sign the contract to the time the doll or bear is available in stores.

Still, designing for a manufacturer can be rewarding, both in terms of publicity and finances. You will probably make more money by selling your designs to manufacturers than you would selling your original dolls and bears. You will also save on the costs associated with advertising, publicity and processing orders. In addition, if you are tired of making hundreds and hundreds of creations just to fill orders, you will have the chance to spend more time on the designing end.

LANDING INTEREST IN YOUR WORK

Manufacturers' reps have probably already seen your work at shows. They are constantly looking for new designers. Sometimes they pose as collectors. They may make an appointment to talk to you privately at a show or take a business card and call you later. Sometimes reps will become interested in your work after seeing it in a shop or magazine. They may purchase a doll or bear from you, or from a shop, and call you later about the possibility of producing a design.

If manufacturers are not coming to you, go to them! If you attend trade shows, such as Toy Fair, manufacturers' reps are often in attendance. You will usually get a list of exhibitors before the show. Even if a particular manufacturer is not exhibiting, reps from that company may be in attendance looking for new designers. If you contact them before the show, you may be able to set up an appointment to show them a prototype. At Toy Fair in 1986, Carol-Lynn made appointments to show the same prototype to two different manufacturers. Turned out they were located exactly across the aisle from each other! So much for clandestine activities.

Another option is to send a press kit (see chapter 8). First, make sure the manufacturer accepts unsolicited submissions. Some do not. Others have their own design staff but still accept unsolicited submissions occasionally from outside designers. Others only produce work by doll and bear artists like you who want to have their designs mass-produced.

Before sending your press kit, call and ask for the product development manager or someone in the submissions department. Once you have them on the phone, ask what they need in terms of a submission, and ask whether they would be willing to sign a nondisclosure statement before you send them your press kit. If they agree, send the nondisclosure agreement first, and when it is signed and returned, send the press kit. (For more information on nondisclosure statements, see the section below.) Include photos of the doll(s) or bear(s) you would like to have mass-produced and a cover letter. The cover letter should include the name of the product development manager or other appropriate person.

On the next page is a sample cover letter to include with your nondisclosure statement.

If you do not hear from the company within two weeks, call again to see if the product development manager plans to sign the statement. Always include a self-addressed, stamped envelope with such a letter.

Once the nondisclosure statement has been signed, send your press kit, along with another cover letter. An example letter is on page 145.

Eventually, if the company is interested, you will either be asked for an interview or asked to send a prototype of your doll or bear.

If you are approached by a manufacturer or looking for a manufacturer to mass-produce your work, go back to your research. Find out what the manufacturer is currently producing. Will your doll or bear fit in with the manufacturer's current product line? How does the manufacturer sell and advertise? What kind of reputation does the manufacturer have?

Never begin contract negotiations until you have talked to other artists who have worked with the manufacturer. Some contracts have clauses in them saying you can't reveal the terms they offer you if you sign them. That's so artists will not go around comparing deals. While another artist's contract may forbid her from discussing finances with you, she will usually be able to tell you if she was satisfied overall, how she was treated, and if she felt her payment was fair. Again, this points to the importance of networking. How else will you get to know other artists who can offer this kind of advice?

PROTECTING YOUR IDEAS

What can prevent a company from going with a concept you show them and never paying for it? It has happened to Carol-Lynn, and many other teddy bear and doll artists out there, so be careful. Unfortunately, ideas and concepts are not protected by copyright law, only the artistic expression of them. However, you can prevent a manufacturer from using a pattern or mold you provide as a prototype. The best way to protect yourself is by asking the manufacturer to sign a nondisclosure statement before you even explain a concept or show a design. A nondisclosure statement simply states that you are about to reveal to the other party certain valuable information and designs which are confidential, and that the other party agrees to keep confidential everything you say and show until you sign a contract.

You can put together a nondisclosure statement using your own words and present it to the person with whom you meet to discuss an idea or prototype. Many artists choose to have a lawyer versed in copyright laws

COVER LETTER FOR NONDISCLOSURE
STATEMENT

Dear [name of product development manager],

As we discussed on the telephone on April 12, I am sending a nondisclosure statement for you to sign and return to me in the enclosed self-addressed, stamped envelope. When I receive this signed statement, I will send a press kit which includes photos of my one-of-a-kind mohair teddy bear, Caroline. I am hoping to have my Caroline design mass-produced, and believe that she would fit the image and goals of your company. Thank you for your consideration. If you need to reach me, feel free to call me at home at (555) 555-5555.
    Sincerely,

[Your signature here]

[Your name here]

COVER LETTER FOR PRESS KIT

Dear [name of product development manager],

Thank you for signing the nondisclosure statement that will allow me to show you my design for Caroline, a one-of-a-kind mohair teddy bear that I would like to have mass-produced and marketed by your company. I have enclosed my press kit, along with three photos of Caroline. She is a 10″ bear with a contemplative expression who wears an originally designed red velvet dress with lace. If you are interested in talking to me about this design, please call me at (555) 555-5555. I look forward to hearing from you!
   Sincerely,

[Your signature here]

[Your name here]

put such a statement together for them.

It's corporate policy, however, for employees of many big companies to refuse to sign such a statement. Sometimes companies will go so far as to ask you to sign a counteragreement that basically states, "I am showing you my original designs and you have no obligation to keep any of this to yourself. If a product you design comes close to my concept, too bad for me. I won't complain or take legal action. I'm showing you my design on the chance that you will pay money for it." This is called a submission form or a waiver form and is getting far too common.

GUARDING YOUR RIGHTS

So a manufacturer wants to reproduce your design. Now what? It's time to begin contract negotiations, and during this process, you will have to be careful about guarding your rights. As opposed to the idea and concepts on which they are based, your executed designs are called intellectual property and are automatically covered by copyright when you create them. Those who want to reproduce your designs want to acquire as much control as possible. They will try to take whatever they can get. It's their business. If you have the notion that the toy business is warm and fuzzy, think again.

You, on the other hand, want to retain as much control and as many rights to your doll or bear design as possible. You will be offered contracts with terms that you may not understand. Do not sign anything until you show it to someone who understands contracts and copyright law, preferably a lawyer versed in copyright law. It is well worth it to pay a copyright lawyer to look over your contract.

If you remember nothing else from this chapter, remember *never* to sign a licensing agreement if it sounds like a "work-for-hire" agreement. If you do, you have just given away your copyright. Licensing involves parts of the law that most of us don't understand well. This is why the companies have the upper hand: They understand the ins and outs in negotiating and writing in codicils that seem to say one thing and say another instead. Some companies count on artists being naive. If you see a contract that says you are selling all rights or work-for-hire, red lights should be flashing in your brain.

Signing such a work-for-hire contract means you give the company the copyright and all control and rights to your design. The buyer of your work is treated as the creator by the copyright law. You have lost everything except the five hundred dollars you were paid for that creation. The buyer can then do whatever he wants with your work, including printing its image on coffee mugs and plates if he wants to do so. Some companies are sneaky about this. Be careful! Never sign a contract until you read and understand everything in it.

If you work for a firm as an employee, work-for-hire usually is in force. This means everything you design while you work as a salaried employee for the firm belongs to it, and not to you. In addition, if you sign a work-for-hire agreement, the company has no obligation to let anyone know you designed the work. They can say they did it, because they bought the right to do so.

THE INS AND OUTS OF LICENSING

When you license something, you agree to transfer rights to use your work to someone else. The owner of the work is the licensor. The image is the licensed property. The person or company getting rights is the licensee. The terms for the use of the image, including territory and the length of time the license lasts, are called the grant of the license. You are not selling your work. The license does not transfer title to it. You are selling the right to use your design for a specific purpose in a specific place for a specific time period. In exchange, the licensee pays the licensor a royalty.

PAYMENT

A royalty is a percentage of the monies received when the product sells. Be aware that royalties can be based on a wholesale or retail price, and this makes a big difference in the money you get. Six percent of retail is better than 8 percent of wholesale. Sometimes an artist receives an advance, which is an amount of money paid to the artist in anticipation of sales, and which will be taken out of the royalties earned later. Ask for a complete accounting of your royalties quarterly, with indications on how many units were sold and for how much each, not just a final cost in a lump sum.

You can license your design for specific purposes: for manufacture, for T-shirt reproduction rights, for figurine rights. Don't give your licensee all rights when you know she will never use them.

THE TERM OF AGREEMENT

Be sure to limit the amount of time the license is valid. This is generally called the term of agreement. This will allow you to have the design reproduced by another company if you are not satisfied. If you are satisfied, you will usually have the chance to renew the contract. It's better to be safe than sorry.

EXCLUSIVE VS. NONEXCLUSIVE RIGHTS

You can give your licensee exclusive or nonexclusive rights to market the design. Nonexclusive means you can design for other companies while you are working with this company. Unless you are willing to wait until your contract is up to sell your designs to other manufacturers, your best bet is to fight for nonexclusive rights. Also, be sure to state in your contract that the other party cannot sublicense your work (which means to allow someone else to reproduce your design for a payment).

WHAT MUST YOU SUPPLY THE MANUFACTURER?

Your contract should also state what you will be responsible for supplying to the manufacturer. You may be asked to supply the original doll or bear, the pattern or mold for that doll or bear, patterns for clothing or doll bodies, etc. Be sure you are clear on this from the beginning so there are no surprises later in the process.

NAME AND COPYRIGHT

Demand your name and copyright be on every piece of advertising, packaging, and each tag, especially the sewn-in tag. Your name should be incised on the back of the doll's head. Make sure your copyright is indicated in your name, not the company's, prominently and permanently. Make sure your name will also be associated with the doll or bear in all advertising and sales.

PRODUCTION STANDARDS

Ask for the right to reject the product if it falls below your standards while in production. You do not want a product out there with your name on it if you are not happy. Most contracts will specify what rights the artist has in terms of approval. It is advisable to ask for the right of final approval. This way, you see the doll or bear in its final version, and you have the final say about whether you want that doll or bear to be put on the market.

MANUFACTURING, DISTRIBUTION AND SALES

Your contract should state that you will receive royalties and sales information on all dolls or bears produced under this contract for all countries in which your work is sold. Further, make sure the contract states what happens to your prototype when production ceases. It should return to you, as should your original molds.

How will your dolls or bears be marketed? Find out the marketing methods planned for your project and get them in writing. Your work

TIPS FOR NEGOTIATING YOUR CONTRACT

- Don't agree to exclusivity.
- Don't sell "all your rights" or "work for hire."
- Do be as specific as you can about exactly which rights you license and for how long.
- Do understand how much money you're getting in terms of royalties and what the percentage is based on.
- Do state in your contract that the other party cannot sublicense your work (which means to allow someone else to do your design for a payment).
- Do ask for final approval of your product.
- Do ask for the right to buy as many of your product as you want at the manufacturer's cost.
- Do demand your name and copyright be on every piece of advertising, packaging, and each tag, especially the sewn-in tag or incised name on the back of the doll's head. Make sure your copyright is indicated in your name, not the company's, prominently and permanently.
- Do ask for a dozen free examples of your commercially produced work.
- Do ask for a complete accounting of your royalties quarterly, with indications on how many units were sold in which country, and for how much each, not just a final cost in a lump sum.
- Do ask for the right to reject the product if it falls below your standards while in production.
- Do ask for reimbursement for all costs involved in promotional travel for your product and a *per diem* to be paid you each day to compensate for your lost work time.
- Do not sign an agreement binding you to an extensive promotional tour.

could be sold through direct mail, in shops, at shows, through magazine advertisements, on television, even on the Internet. Make sure you can live with their plans.

Does the contract bind you to a promotional tour. How many days a year, where and at whose expense? It may sound glamorous, but it will get old fast, especially since you can't work while on the road. Ask for reimbursement for all costs involved in promotional travel for your product and a per diem sum to be paid you each day to compensate for your lost work time. This should cut down on your public appearances. The more time you spend on the road making money for the company, the less time you'll spend in your studio making money for yourself.

You can see why you need a written contract in this business. One company that wanted to produce Carol-Lynn's bear Yetta said it never signed a contract. It said it believed in handshake agreements. Some people believe in the tooth fairy. If it's not written down, it doesn't count. If it's not written down in easy-to-understand language, it's not good enough. If it's written down and you hate it, cross it out and write in something else. Carol-Lynn has completely redone contracts, taking out everything she did not like, which was almost everything.

Does going commercial still sound seductive? Then go for it! Good luck!

If you cannot locate a copyright attorney in your area, go to the local library where you will find big city telephone books. The yellow pages are available on CD-ROM for a reasonable cost at most computer software shops.

You can contact the national headquarters of Volunteer Lawyers for the Arts, One East 53rd St., Sixth Floor, New York, New York 10022, or call (212) 319-2787. Local chapters can be found through your state's Bar Association. These organizations specialize in helping artists and can help you find a lawyer in your area. They may even be able to offer free information over the phone, although it is best to talk to a lawyer specifically versed in copyright laws.

CHAPTER SIXTEEN

How to Keep 'Em Coming Back

*O*nce you've made that first sale to a collector, a shop, or a manufacturing company, it's easy to sit back and count your money without giving the sale a second thought. Don't fall into this trap. The only way to make money selling your dolls and teddy bears is by getting loyal customers to come back for more.

THE PERSONAL TOUCH

The secret is T.L.C.: tender loving care. Everyone likes thoughtful people. You probably show those you care about that you are thinking of them in special ways. Do you send your favorite aunt a card on Mother's Day, or send a thank-you note when you receive a gift, even if it's something you hated?

Probably. The same philosophy works with your customers. They want to know you are thinking of them. If they don't hear from you, they may forget about you. Remember the chapter on name recognition. Do anything you can to remind past customers you are still around, still making dolls and bears they will probably love.

Each time a customer buys a doll or bear from you, send a handwritten thank-you note. This personal touch will be much appreciated and fondly remembered. Add all buyers to your mailing list so they will receive your postcards reminding them of upcoming shows. If you have time, you may want to send flyers or newsletters to those on your mailing list. These newsletters could include information about new editions, upcoming shows and awards. Doll and teddy bear collectors love to be kept up-to-date.

Send past customers holiday greeting cards. Nearly all businesses send greeting cards around the holidays to their clients, and this is a good way to show you care. One highly successful artist sends birthday cards on the anniversary of the day the customer bought a bear from her. This works well for her and leads to increased sales. Remember what we said about marketing yourself as well as your dolls and bears? Collectors are more apt to buy from someone who seems to take a personal interest in them.

SPECIAL OFFERS

Loyal customers deserve special offers. If you can afford to give discounts on a second, third, or fourth doll or bear that a collector purchases from you—or give a shop a break on their third or fourth order—do so as an act of goodwill. Even small discounts, such as a few dollars off, are good incentives.

Other businesses offer special services for preferred customers, with great results. If you can't afford to lower your prices for multiple orders, consider offering special orders only to repeat customers. Give these customers the option of purchasing portrait dolls or custom-made bears, or give prior customers the first shot at purchasing limited editions. Even if you're sure you will never sell out an edition, your prior customers don't need to know this—they will feel it a privilege that you are giving them the first chance to buy.

BEING CONSIDERATE

Good old-fashioned politeness goes a long way. Spend time with *all* your customers at shows, not just the big spenders. Don't judge them by their clothing—a big spender is just as likely to be wearing torn jeans as a three-piece suit. Never act as if a collector is lucky to have your time. Winning an award or having a feature article written about you does not entitle you to act like royalty. This kind of an attitude will get you nowhere with collectors.

If you want to win a second order from a customer, the first order must go smoothly. Be timely. Get orders out as promptly as possible. If you cannot get an order out as planned, call and explain why. Do everything you can to make sure the collector or shop owner is satisfied. She will undoubtedly tell others about your work.

Keep commitments. If you say you will be at a show, a lecture, a work-shop or any other public appearance, be there, and be there on time. Loyal collectors will travel to see you, and they will be disheartened if you do not show up. You will also foster good relations with show promoters and organizers this way, and they, too, can become customers, or at least recommend your work to others.

KEEPING YOUR PRODUCT LINE FRESH

Yes, there are collectors out there with hundreds of Barbie dolls, but collectors of artist-made creations want new concepts. They do not want to see the same old doll at your booth, year after year, with different hair colors and complexions, or the same bear with different costumes. If you want them to keep buying, you have to keep your product line fresh.

Don't get stuck in a rut. Try something new. Keep designing. And let new customers know about your new designs. Keep them updated. If you have a large collector following at one of your shows, why not unveil a new limited edition at this show? This will make them sure to visit your booth.

FINAL ADVICE

It's not easy to get your foot in the door in the doll or bear business. Even more difficult to stay in and keep your chin up through the rough seasons when you're sure you'll never sell another original doll or bear.

When that happens, get out this book. Skim through it again. Be honest. Are you doing everything you can to market and sell your work?

People may tell you that there are just too many artists and too many shows out there. Don't buy into this idea. The more widespread and successful our business becomes, the larger the collector base will become.

Our product speaks a silent, emotive language understandable to buyers worldwide. There's still plenty of room for an artist who creates quality work and conducts business in a professional manner. Sure, the market is challenging. It's full of problems. Tackle the challenges. Solve the problems. Turn negatives into positives, failures into successes. Believe in yourself and in your work, and try not to dwell on the "bad stuff."

Your attitude, whether bad, or good, will affect every aspect of your business. Even though you think you're hiding your pessimism, it's going to affect your work, your relationships with customers and with your family and friends, and your "bottom line." People seek out rainbows and avoid mud puddles.

Do you realize how blessed you are to be working at something about which you are passionate? Have you any idea how envious the other 95 percent of the population is of you, of your perceived talent and freedom, and of your courageous choice to try to make a living through your art?

Your customers wish they, like you, could do what they really love for a living.

The sentence above contains the Real Secret of this book.

If you want to be successful in selling your artwork, you must work from, and with, love. Cynicism and hard-nosed mercenary goals will shine through your work, as will your joy and excitement. Your customers can, and will, pick up on your mind-set, your attitudes, in a hundred nonverbal ways.

So, consider your motives. If they're in the right place, then so are you. Then, consider your heart.

Are you in love with what you're doing? Do you get pleasure, a psychic and emotional high you need and can get from nowhere else, from creating a sculpture from clay—one promising to come to life and breathe? Do you feel your heart melting with a gently parental joy as you finish the face of your bear, and struggle with emotional pangs when your "brainchild" finds a buyer?

Are you constantly surprised when you thought you'd spent only an hour at work, to discover the dawn spilling into your workroom? Have you forgotten to eat, to sleep, to clean the house because the doll or teddy bear inside you demanded *right then* to be born?

If you want to be successful as a doll or bear artist, your work must fill a burning spot in your soul. It must be what you absolutely want—no, need—to do. If this is so, then approach the field with love and passion.

Love yourself, love your work, love your customer. The word will get around.

And your passion for what you're doing will give you the patience and the persistence to learn skills you need to earn a living selling your dolls and teddy bears.

How do we know?

We've been there.

Hold onto that love, and follow the road map within these covers. Welcome to the greatest group of people you will ever meet, the longest hours you will ever work, and the greatest joy you will ever achieve from a profession!

The journey's not always easy, but you can make it.

And when you do, we'll be waiting with open arms to welcome you!

INDEX

More Great Books
for Collectors and Crafters!

The Doll Sourcebook—Bring your dolls and supplies as close as the telephone with this unique sourcebook of retailers, artists, restorers, appraisers and more! Each listing contains extensive information—from addresses and phone numbers to business hours and product lines. *#70325/$22.99/352 pages/176 b&w illus./paperback*

The Teddy Bear Sourcebook: For Collectors and Crafters—Discover the most complete treasury of bear information stuffed between covers. You'll turn here whenever you need to find sellers of bear making supplies, major manufacturers of teddy bears, teddy bear shows, auctions and contests, museums that house teddy bear collections and much more. *#70294/$18.99/356 pages/202 illus./paperback*

The Crafts Supply Sourcebook: A Comprehensive Shop-by-Mail Guide, 4th Edition—Turn here to find the materials you need—from specialty tools and the hardest-to-find accessories, to clays, doll parts, patterns, quilting machines and hundreds of other items! Listings organized by area of interest make it quick and easy! *#70344/$18.99/320 pages/paperback*

Painting Houses, Cottages and Towns on Rocks—Turn ordinary rocks into charming cottages, country churches and Victorian mansions! Accomplished artist Lin Wellford shares 11 fun, inexpensive, step-by-step projects that are sure to please. *#30823/$21.99/128 pages/398 color illus./paperback*

Handmade Jewelry: Simple Steps to Creating Wearable Art—Create unique and wearable pieces of art—and have fun doing it! 42 step-by-step jewelry-making projects are at your fingertips—from necklaces and earrings, to pins and barrettes. Plus, no experience, no fancy equipment and no expensive materials are required! *#30820/$21.99/128 pages/126 color, 30 b&w illus./paperback*

How to Start Making Money With Your Crafts—Launch a rewarding crafts business with this guide that starts with the basics—from creating marketable products to setting the right prices—and explores all the exciting possibilities. End-of-chapter quizzes, worksheets, ideas and lessons learned by successful crafters are included to increase your learning curve. *#70302/$18.99/176 pages/35 b&w illus./paperback*

Dried Flowers: Colors for Every Room in the House—Create exquisite arrangements to match any room or color scheme! With this versatile and easy-to-use reference, you'll discover the full range of available flower types, as well as step-by-step projects and a gallery of arrangements to inspire your work! *#30701/$27.99/144 pages/4-color throughout*

Stencil Source Book 2—Add color and excitement to fabrics, furniture, walls and more with over 200 original motifs that can be used again and again! Idea-packed chapters will help you create dramatic color schemes and themes to enhance your home in hundreds of ways. *#30730/$22.99/144 pages/300 illus.*

The Complete Book of Silk Painting—Create fabulous fabric art—everything from clothing to pillows to wall hangings. You'll learn every aspect of silk painting in this step-by-step guide, including setting up a workspace, necessary materials and fabrics and specific silk painting techniques. *#30362/$26.99/128 pages/4-color throughout*

Fabric Sculpture: The Step-By-Step Guide & Showcase—Discover how to transform fabrics into 3-dimensional images. Seven professional fabric sculptors demonstrate projects that illustrate their unique approaches and methods for creating images from fabric. The techniques—covered in easy, step-by-step illustration and instruction—include quilting, thread work, applique and soft sculpture. *#30687/$29.99/160 pages/300+ color illus.*

Decorative Wreaths & Garlands—Discover stylish, yet simple-to-make wreaths and garlands. These 20 original designs use fabrics and fresh and dried flowers to add color and personality to any room, and charm to special occasions. Clear instructions are accompanied by step-by-step photographs to ensure that you create a perfect display every time. *#30696/$19.99/96 pages/175 color illus.*

The Complete Flower Arranging Book—An attractive, up-to-date guide to creating more than 100 beautiful arrangements with fresh and dried flowers, illustrated with step-by-step demonstrations. *#30405/$24.95/192 pages/300+ color illus.*

The Complete Flower Craft Book—Discover techniques for drying fresh flowers and seedheads, creating arrangements to suit all seasons and occasions, making silk flowers, potpourri, bath oil and more! This guide is packed with photographs, tips and step-by-step instructions to give you a bouquet of ideas and inspiration! *#30589/$24.95/144 pages/275 color illus.*

Jewelry & Accessories: Beautiful Designs to Make and Wear—Discover how to make unique jewelry out of papier maché, wood, leather, cloth and metals. You'll learn how to create a hand-painted wooden brooch, a silk-painted hair slide, a paper and copper necklace and much more! Fully illustrated with step-by-step instructions. *#30680/$17.99/128 pages/150 color illus./paperback*

The Art of Painting Animals on Rocks—Discover how a dash of paint can turn humble stones into charming "pet rocks." This hands-on easy-to-follow book offers a menagerie of fun—and potentially profitable—stone animal projects. 11 examples, complete with material list, photos of the finished piece and patterns will help you create a forest of fawns, rabbits, foxes and other adorable critters. *#30606/$21.99/144 pages/250 color illus./paperback*

Decorative Boxes to Create, Give and Keep—Craft beautiful boxes using techniques including embroidery, stenciling, lacquering, gilding, shellwork, decoupage and many others. Step-by-step instructions and photographs detail every project. *#30638/$15.95/128 pages/4-color throughout/paperback*

Elegant Ribboncraft—Over 40 ideas for exquisite ribbon-craft— hand-tied bows, floral garlands, ribbon embroidery and more. Various techniques are employed—including folding, pleating, plaiting, weaving, embroidery, patchwork, quilting, applique and decoupage. All projects are complete with step-by-step instructions and photographs. *#30697/$16.99/128 pages/130+ color illus.*

Paint Craft—Discover great ideas for enhancing your home, wardrobe and personal items. You'll see how to master the basics of mixing and planning colors, how to print with screen and linoleum to create your own stationery, how to enhance old glassware and pottery pieces with unique patterns and motifs and much more! *#30678/$16.99/144 pages/200 color illus./paperback*

Nature Craft—Dozens of step-by-step nature craft projects to create, including dried flower garlands, baskets, corn dollies, potpourri and more. Bring the outdoors inside with these wonderful projects crafted with readily available natural materials. *#30531/$16.99/144 pages/200 color illus./paperback*

Paper Craft—Dozens of step-by-step paper craft projects to make, including greeting cards, boxes and desk sets, jewelry and pleated paper blinds. If you have ever worked with or wanted to work with paper you'll enjoy these attractive, fun-to-make projects. *#30530/$16.95/144 pages/200 color illus./paperback*

Everything You Ever Wanted to Know About Fabric Painting—Discover how to create beautiful fabrics! You'll learn how to set up work space, choose materials, plus the ins and outs of tie-dye, screen printing, woodgraining, marbling, cyanotype and more! *#30625/$21.99/128 pages/4-color throughout/paperback*

Holiday Fun Year-Round With Dian Thomas—Discover how to turn mere holiday observances into opportunities to exercise imagination and turn the festivity all the way up. You'll find suggestions for a memorable New Year's celebration, silly April Fool's Day pranks, recipes and ideas for a Labor Day family get-together, creative Christmas giving and much more! *#70300/$19.99/144 pages/150 color illus./paperback*
